D1127798

MY STORY

Mohammed bin Rashid Al Maktoum

50 MEMORIES
FROM FIFTY YEARS
OF SERVICE

MY STORY

First Edition: February 2019

THE EXECUTIVE OFFICE

© All rights are reserved by The Executive Office
of His Highness Sheikh Mohammed bin Rashid Al Maktoum

Published By
Explorer Publishing & Distribution
PO Box 34275, Dubai, UAE
+971 (4) 340 8805
info@ask**explorer**.com
ask**explorer**.com

National Media Council Approval Number MC-02-01-0969783

ISBN 978-1-78596-500-5

All rights reserved. No reproduction of any part of the present publication
is allowed, nor is it allowed to archive or copy it in any way whatsoever,
whether electronically, mechanically or by copying or saving, or
otherwise without obtaining the permission of the Executive Office of
His Highness Sheikh Mohammed bin Rashid Al Maktoum.

Image Credits
Cover: Za'abeel Studio; p14 A. Abbas/Magnum Photos; p50 Explorer Publishing;
p147 Harry Todd/Fox Photos/Getty Images; p200 Tim Peake/ESA/NASA via Getty Images;
p204 Rustam Azmi/Getty Images; p244 Louai Bechara/AFP/Getty Images;
p246 Rabih Moghrabi/AFP/Getty Images; p268 Mychele Daniau/AFP/Getty Images

Emiratis may choose to refer
to this record for evidence of
who we used to be, as well as
how we established one of the
most dynamic and successful
countries on Earth

Mohammed bin Rashid Al Maktoum

Introduction

For the last 50 years, it has been my honour and privilege to serve the people of the UAE. In half a century, Dubai has grown from a small, bustling port on the Gulf to a truly global city boasting a population that includes almost every nationality on Earth. In less than two years' time my nation will celebrate its golden jubilee – the 50th anniversary of the accord that brought the UAE into being as a proud and independent nation.

This book shares some of the highlights of my journey, revisiting many of the vivid memories of the people and events that have shaped a great deal of my life and that were often to shape the life of our country. Accordingly, I am marking my 50 years of work with a book that contains 50 chapters. It is for my fellow citizens that I have recorded these personal milestones in the hope that they will provide some insight and inspiration to future generations.

This is, and only can be, an incomplete record – just a small part of documenting the history of our beloved nation, preserving it for those to come. In the years that follow, Emiratis may choose to refer to this record for evidence of who we used to be, as well as how we established one of the most dynamic and successful countries on Earth. Our only wish is for coming generations to see how hard we have worked to build the future that they will inherit.

I have recorded events as I recall them and with the aid of diaries, poems and other notes that I made at the time. These reminiscences, then, I have dashed down as time has permitted, in the hope that we can build on our past as we seek to shape our future.

We embarked on our journey 50 years ago, guided by the words: "Work sincerely and soon God and the faithful will observe your efforts."

The road ahead of us remains a long one and still our vision – shaped for the benefit of our people and our nation – has yet to be fulfilled. We always seek the best in people and aim to develop their potential for everybody's benefit. Crises will not stop us, obstacles will not slow us. Nor will we hesitate or be halted by doubt.

In these simple words, I hope you will find a little wisdom and the reflection of my love for our nation and my brothers and sisters across the UAE and across the world. I share them with you, perhaps to help inspire, or teach our young, the Arab youth and youth everywhere. You, like us, seek to build a better homeland, to spread hope for the future and for the future of our world.

As a public servant, I gain joy and energy from the happiness of my people and from their satisfaction and safety, as I know they, in turn, wish for my family and children what they wish for their own.

In the Name of God, the Most Gracious, the Most Merciful
Your Brother,

Mohammed bin Rashid Al Maktoum

Contents

01

From Where We Started to Where We Are Today

The day of December 6th, 2017, is one that I remember particularly well. I was up early but did not have breakfast until after 11am because most of the morning was devoted to a new and very exciting project – one that would lead our nation in a new and unexpected direction. I love to set challenges because I believe development and evolution come from demanding the 'impossible'. Setting one's sights on the horizon is all very well, but it is by looking beyond it that we humans fully engage our imagination to inspire true achievements.

This new objective was genuinely extraordinary and I was keen to use it to fire the people's imagination. I wanted the message to be clear: nothing is impossible, no barrier can stand in the way of our nation and our will to succeed.

In the home of my grandfather Sheikh Saeed bin Maktoum Al Maktoum in 2018

We had worked quietly on developing this project for several years. We had formed our team, built our capacity and established international partnerships. We had set out on a new and ambitious path to advance our capabilities in the field of science. Later that day, I announced the project to more than 15 million social media followers – to send the first UAE astronauts to the International Space Station.

This was the culmination of more than a decade's work to create an integrated ecosystem of space sciences, spacecraft engineering and mission operations. We had already started on our mission to send an unmanned probe to orbit Mars and announced the development of the first city on Earth to simulate our neighbouring planet's climatic conditions – the Mars 2117 project has the long-term goal of establishing an inhabited and sustainable city on the Red Planet.

We had developed the first Arab satellite manufacturing programme with the capability of designing, building and managing our own satellites, and cultivated a fast-growing community of Emirati satellite engineers, space scientists and technicians. Now we would send our astronauts to conduct scientific experiments aboard the International Space Station – experiments designed by UAE academic institutions to truly further our scientific knowledge and understanding. We had solid goals for our astronauts to achieve beyond merely embarking on a journey. I watched people's reactions to the news and witnessed an upsurge of pride and happiness in our nation. Young people in particular were caught up with the idea. We had a new summit, I knew, but I also knew this was just the beginning. On that beautiful morning, with our sights set on outer space, my mind went back to my own beginnings. How far had we come?

I love to set challenges
because I believe development
and evolution come from
demanding the 'impossible'

Launch of the Emirates Mars Mission in 2015

Sheikh Saeed bin Maktoum Al Maktoum's house in Al Shindagha

I was born in the house of my grandfather, Sheikh Saeed, in Al Shindagha. I recall the clay walls interspersed with coral, allowing the fresh air to pass, the low-roofed rooms, the courtyard and my parents' and siblings' bedrooms. I remember my grandfather with his white beard and beaming face. My memory of him is of a man who won respect for his good heart and strong faith. In many ways, Dubai's story starts with him for he helped the city diversify and find new markets. He opened Dubai to new trade routes and unlocked the door to prosperity. But his greatest achievement was his relationship with his people. He loved them and they loved him, very deeply. They said he used to wake up before the *Fajr* (dawn) prayer, go to a distant well, fill a large bucket with water and bring it to the mosque so that the worshippers could perform their *Wudu* (ablutions), prior to prayer. My grandfather never judged, nor ruled with fear, but with utmost love and compassion. His *majlis* was where he shared his wisdom and heard the grievances of his fellow citizens, making sure that justice prevailed. Maybe this is why he came into my thoughts on the day we announced we would send the first Emiratis into outer space, for mercy and love can never be forgotten, nor erased by time.

I was almost nine years old on the day he passed away, breathing his last shortly after *Fajr*, with my father at his side. I remember the lamentation of women and the crying of men. I would never have thought these proud men would cry. I remember the flags lowered to half-mast and the large crowds bidding farewell at his final resting place. I remember his image imprinted on my memory – before *Fajr*, with his bucket of water at the mosque waiting for his people. Oh, Abu Rashid, you taught us how to serve people! May God have mercy on your soul.

02

A Lesson Among All Lessons, from the King of Kings

The anniversary marking 2,500 years since the foundation of the Persian Empire in 1971

Dominion belongs to God alone. Greatness belongs to God alone. He is the king of all kings. He endures and all else perishes. No flaunter shall last forever, for greatness belongs to God alone. As a poet once said:

> Where are the crowned kings of Yemen,
>> and where are their jewel-studded diadems and crowns?
> Where are the buildings Shaddad raised in Iran,
>> and where is the empire the Sasanians ruled in Persia?
> Where is the gold Qarun once possessed,
>> and where are 'Ad and Shaddad and Qahtan?

It is said that the Kings of the Earth are four: Nimrod, Bakht Nasr, Dhul-Qarnayn, and Solomon, who is the greatest of them all. It is said that a man once tried to stop a king's procession to talk to him, but the king's guards stepped in and held him back.

He shouted out, "Oh King! The prophet Solomon was stopped by an ant. He came to a stop and talked to it. Am I even more contemptible than an ant? And are you dearer to God than Solomon?"

The king jumped off his horse, went to the man and talked to him.

I have been reminded of these lines frequently by the events of recent years, which have also taken me back to a key formative experience of my youth. After my father, Sheikh Rashid, became Ruler of Dubai, I started to accompany him on foreign appointments. I joined him on a visit to meet Mohammad Reza Pahlavi, the Shah of Iran – the 'Emperor' or *Shahenshah* ('King of Kings') as he later styled himself while sitting on the Peacock Throne.

I was 11 years old. I did not understand much of such dizzying greatness, nor of the trappings employed by kings to distinguish themselves from their people.

Still to this day, I remain puzzled by the need of some leaders to instil into their people the illusion of such class distinction – the idea that they are of the chosen few, moving further away from the citizenry until they are isolated in their own self-imposed prisons.

I saw this dazzling world again in 1971 when I visited the Shah in my own right to celebrate the 2,500th anniversary of the founding of the Persian Empire. The Iranians spent more than $100 million, a colossal

The legendary celebration of the 2,500th anniversary of the founding of the Persian Empire in 1971

> ## 66
> ## Dominion belongs to God alone. Greatness belongs to God alone
> ## 99

amount at the time and equivalent to around $750 million today, on a grandiose ceremony in the ancient Iranian city of Persepolis. Heads of state from around the world were invited to this ceremony. Almost 60 tents covered more than 160 acres, in the middle of which three huge royal pavilions were set in a lush garden, specifically built for the purpose. French chefs prepared dishes of peacock meat, served to us on Limoges porcelain china, drinks were offered in Baccarat crystal glasses. Thousands of soldiers were present, dressed in historical Persian costumes to reflect the royal splendour.

I enjoyed the ceremony, the shows and meeting the guests and attendees. Yet I also saw the villages of Iran, the poor and needy living on the streets. It reinforced my impression of that first visit as a young man – that the glittering opulence enjoyed by the leader came at the expense of the people.

At the time, Dubai was still a small town of limited means and life was hard for many people, but my father did not live in a palace. He started his day early in the morning, meeting people and following up on projects with workers and engineers, consulting with and advising the public, having a simple lunch with his guests. He had an office above the wharf on Dubai Creek, where dhows would unload their goods. He was a modest man; his visitors sometimes thought he was just an employee. Project engineers even called him 'The Foreman', given his frequent and constant follow-up visits. My father's relationship with the Shah was good, of course, and he visited him on many occasions but a stark contrast existed between the two men's lives.

After the ceremony, the paradox never left my mind. I could never imagine Sheikh Rashid sitting on the Peacock Throne and putting a crown on his head. He was far from this, closer to simplicity, closer to the people. Yes, the secret to being a successful leader is to remain close to your people. This is the greatest of all lessons.

I wished then that the Shah had looked around him with a little more wisdom. Over the previous two decades, several thrones and monarchies – which we had thought immutable – had fallen all around him. In 1952, the Egyptian army had led a military coup against King Farouk, who was forced to abdicate and flee into exile. In 1958, Iraq's King Faisal was murdered along with other members of his family. Four years later, Imam Muhammad Al Badr was deposed in Yemen, and in 1969, King Idris of Libya was overthrown in a military coup led by Muammar Gaddafi. Had these historical precedents gone unnoticed?

The King of Kings paid little attention to such rapid changes and relied on British and American support instead of his people's love. He was distant from them, preoccupied with his palaces and preposterous lifestyle. In 1979, just eight years after this huge celebration, the King of Kings fell from the Peacock Throne in the wake of riots and demonstrations that took place in his country, leading to an Islamic revolution mounted by the *mullahs*. Lacking even the support of his former friends, the Shah fled his country for Egypt.

As so often in countries ravaged by revolution, the revolutionaries then became 'kings' of a different sort, just naming their countries 'republics' instead of 'monarchies'. Just as with the former kings or emperors, they built majestic palaces for themselves, living remote from the people and surrounding themselves with circles of admirers who would applaud their achievements.

Years later, in 2004, I addressed these latter-day Arab leaders, saying, "You brought about revolution, so now continue to make changes in the economy, construction, reconstruction and provision of a decent life for your people. Change, or else you will be changed. I have witnessed this before and I can see it now coming again."

Unfortunately, they did not listen. Their countries plunged into darkness, revolution, disorder and chaos that only led to further damage. Where is the UAE and where are these countries standing today? Where are Zayed and Rashid and their dream of a Union of United Arab Emirates, and where is the King of Kings and his peers today?

A fundamental difference exists between our governance and that of these countries, namely remaining in close proximity to our people, while maintaining modesty in serving them and ensuring their happiness. This is the simple difference between prosperity and collapse, success and failure, decency and disgrace.

03

Sleeping with Scorpions

I was seven or eight years old when my father started taking me into the desert to visit one of the elders of the Manasir tribe, Humaid bin Amhi, to learn the art of hunting. Humaid did not live near the water like the rest of the *Bedu*, but was far away in the desert with a camel, a falcon, a hunting dog and tents, along with his wife, a woman whose fortitude I still remember with awe today. She had the strength to carry firewood, milk the camels and slaughter and cook the sheep unaided, in addition to all the other falconry and hunting skills she had mastered. I still remember the meal she used to prepare when we were not hunting: a thick bread, baked under coal and ash and eaten with ghee and honey. With it we would drink camel milk. It was a delightful meal that I enjoyed amid the winter desert chill.

With Humaid bin Amhi, one of the elders of the Manasir tribe

My father used to leave me with Humaid for days. I learned from him how to hunt with falcons and dogs, and he taught me the movement, habits and many camouflage tricks of animals. He taught me how a predator hunts and how the weak are beaten down.

For instance, it is useless to try hunting rabbits when they are feeding, because they bolt. They can be caught far more easily when they have gone to ground. In the summer they dig deeper burrows, in winter they will rest among the bushes that poke through the sand. The best way to catch rabbits lies in tracking their movements to their burrows. They can avoid this, however, by jumping very softly – as light as cotton on sand – towards their sleeping places, so as not to leave traces for enemies to follow. Only an expert in such species and their habits, and of the desert and the movement of its sands, can detect such faint tracks.

I also learned a great deal from Humaid about falcons and their tendencies, about hunting dogs and their natures. You can train dogs to hunt wild deer and, at the same time, train them to co-exist with the deer you have raised. You can train a deer to graze with sheep and to have no fear of your hunting dog. Many people, for example, do not know why the *Bedu* always place the falcon on their arm and raise it to eye level. It is because the falcon senses danger if it is lower than another animal: the eagle is the falcon's enemy and strikes from above. This is why a falcon will attack any bird that flies overhead.

After a day of hunting and learning, we used to gather around the fire to dine and talk tirelessly. Those memories of beautiful, passionate and even painful moments are still engraved in my mind.

> ❝
> # Not all that hurts you is evil. Sometimes pain teaches us and protects us
> ❞

The warmth of the bed amid the cold desert is unmatched by anything, anything at all. I used to wake up multiple times during the night to small scorpion stings. The scorpions seemed to be looking for warmth too, in my bed. I would wake up in pain, severe pain. This is when Humaid used to take me close to the fire and put ash on the wound to reduce and absorb the poison. The heat of the ash also relieved the pain, which flooded back as soon as it cooled.

Can you imagine being woken up three or four times a night to such agonising pain? I was always surprised that I was the only one to be stung by scorpions! Yes, the only one!

In time, I found out there were two reasons for this. The first was my fault: I hadn't listened to the *Bedu* advice to check my bed before sleeping in the desert. The second was that Humaid used to collect and put ten to 12 young scorpions in my bed intentionally!

He wanted to build my immunity against deadly scorpion stings. He was right; to this day, I'm still immune to scorpion venom. Not all that hurts you is evil. Sometimes pain teaches us and protects us.

> 66
>
> I dislike gossipers and
> conspirators. They're toxic,
> they incite you to act against
> humanity, destroy group morale,
> undervalue achievements,
> only focus on the negative and
> never see the good in others
>
> 99

A few years ago, I was in the desert chasing a large scorpion, which took cover underneath some small shrubs and turned around on me. I stepped back without paying attention and it stung me hard.

I bandaged my leg and put some ash and hot water on it. I survived the sting, owing to Humaid's simple wisdom and God's mercy.

Desert scorpions are easier to handle than their human counterparts. Desert scorpions look only for warmth at night and, rather than attacking, prefer to leave as the cold starts to recede. They only sting when they sense danger. The human scorpion, however, loves to bite and hurt. It is said that human scorpions dwell on the Earth in the form of gossipers and conspirators, who trouble souls, destroy relationships and subvert the spirit of communities and teams. I dislike gossipers and conspirators. They're toxic, they incite you to act against humanity, destroy group morale, undervalue achievements, only focus on the negative and never see the good in others. They are hypocrites, two-faced people who are driven by envy and jealousy.

One day, a king addressed one of his faithful companions, confronting him with things which had been said about him. When the companion denied having said or done anything, the king vouched for the credibility of his informant. But the companion replied, "Gossipers are never honest", and the king was forced to agree.

A poet once said:

> People talk and
>   talk behind one's back
> He who gossips about others
>   shall never be believed
> As the river flows,
>   this goes unnoticed

It's true: sleeping with desert scorpions is sometimes easier than living with the human ones.

May God have mercy upon your soul, Humaid.

04

My Father, My First Teacher

Sheikh Rashid bin Saeed Al Maktoum

My father Rashid bin Saeed was my first teacher. He was tall and his face was wrinkled, for he never stopped smiling. The lines surrounding his eyes accentuated his considerable stature and gravitas. His voice was calm and warm, as smooth as a breath. Nevertheless, silence fell when he began to speak.

Among the very first moments I will never forget are the times I used to ride with him on his horse. I was not quite three years old when he used to take me with him on his morning ride. My father, the horses and Dubai are my first memories of childhood – ones that will stay with me until the end. Horses symbolise pride, self-esteem, tenderness and strength all at once. So does my father. So does Dubai!

My father sent me to school to learn how to read and write, to learn languages and sciences. He used to take me with him to his meetings, and on his trips and visits to learn more about the ways of the world.

When I was still between four and eight years old, my father taught me a lot about the desert, about how one could live a full life there despite the harshness, scarcity of resources and desolation that might scare off many people. He taught me how to track and read the sand, just as if flipping through a book. He showed me the tracks of camels and said, "Every *Bedouin* can distinguish their own camels by their footprints, even from among hundreds of others!"

When I was young, my father taught me about the tracks of deer, houbara bustard, curlews, scorpions, snakes, wolves, foxes and every other animal inhabiting the desert. He used to say, "You cannot understand an animal without understanding the environment in which it lives and where it belongs. The same applies to humans.

The environment in which they live may make them either angels or devils. One must know the environment in which they grew up."

When he wanted to teach me the art of falconry, he introduced me first to the falcons' food, such as pigeons and shrews, as well as to their predators, like wolves and eagles, and to the diseases that could kill them. In order to get to know a certain animal, one should become familiar with all its qualities including its behaviours, likes and dislikes.

We spent long nights in the desert. We used to build a large fire when the sun set and during the night my father would take me to watch what was happening around us; a whole new world coming to life as so many humans slept. Mornings were the most beautiful, slowly revealing the holes from which scorpions silently crept into your bed. The dogs often woke up during the night if they heard the trip of a gazelle, or detected its scent, and noiselessly set out to catch it. Keeping track of where the dogs had been, of the distance they had travelled and of the heights they had leaped to catch their prey, would determine whether we would be able to hunt the next day or not.

My father taught me how animals react when they see us or each other. For example, the houbara bustard flies towards the sun to blind the hunter, and the rabbit looks for a hiding place, while the gazelle takes advantage of the open space to be able to see an attacker approach. When an animal jumps with its front legs raised, this frantic movement serves as a warning to all. A strategy is required to have access to food in the desert. My father used to say, "When you spend the night hungry, you will learn your lessons more intensely the next morning."

With my father and teacher Sheikh Rashid bin Saeed Al Maktoum

From my father, I learned how to shoot, and I learned how to unload and clean a gun, even before I was eight years old. From him, I learned that leaving weapons unattended is a serious offence, for they might fall into the hands of another, untrained person and thus take innocent lives away.

From my father, I learned how to skin the prey we hunted, cook its meat and, most important, how to cut the meat into ultra-thin slices and dry it in the sun to preserve it for long periods of time.

We used to go hunting with only basic tools and catch almost all the food we needed. My father took great care to hone my observation skills. He would test me at any time, day or night. I grew accustomed to waking in the night to make sure of my position, prepared with all the answers to any related question he might pose. In the car, he would ask me to describe the terrain. He listened to me carefully and corrected me, providing me with a myriad of small but important details that I had missed. While talking to his friends or travelling a rough track at night, he used to turn around, stare at me intensely and ask me which direction we should take – north or south, east or west? My father made sure to teach me about the Earth and its signs, as well as about the signs of the sky. The stars are the compass of the desert, just as much as the oceans. On cloudy nights, we could use the wind and the glow of the moon to guide us. He used to say, "To get lost in the desert is very easy. Remember, the team will always need a leader to show them the way."

Every day, this instinct for survival and reading the ground took root inside me, deeper and deeper until it became a completely natural and

> My father, the horses and
> Dubai are my first memories of
> childhood – ones that will stay
> with me until the end

automatic process. I learned that I must look for the camels' footprints – or even droppings – if I was lost. For some reason, the hoofprints of animals endure longer in the sand than human footprints. Often, learning from the animals may be the only way to survive. Vanity and arrogance do not, therefore, suit those who live in the desert.

Many times, I would venture into the desert with my elder brothers, Maktoum and Hamdan, and their friends. We would take long treks, often without supplies. They trusted my guidance in the wilderness because of what I had learned from our father.

By the time I was eight years old, my father had taught me how to survive in the desert: how to cope with its vermin and animals, with its wolves and deer, with its cold and heat, and its constantly changing moods. Later on, my father also taught me how to live in the city and how to live with people. This was far more complicated.

How cruel and arid can the human jungle be and yet how bountiful is the desert.

05

Latifa:
My First Love

Latifa in Arabic means friendly, kind and supportive. Latifa in Arabic phraseology means to open the heart and soul. Latifa in life was my mother – my heart and soul. Latifa, in reality, was the most wonderful, supportive, softest, kindest and most extraordinary person in my life.

With my brothers, Sheikh Maktoum and Sheikh Hamdan bin Rashid Al Maktoum

Her full name was Latifa bint Hamdan bin Zayed Al Nahyan and her father served as the Ruler of Abu Dhabi from 1912 to 1922. She was the light of my father's life for more than 40 years.

A year after her marriage to Sheikh Rashid, she gave birth to their first daughter, Maryam. The future Ruler of Dubai, Maktoum bin Rashid, was born three years later. A great ceremony was held when Sheikh Maktoum opened his eyes to the world for the very first time.

A few years later, the family welcomed a second son, Hamdan bin Rashid, named after my grandfather Hamdan bin Zayed. My mother gave birth to another son, Marwan; ill fated, he died tragically when young. My mother could hardly bear this great loss. She lived a beautiful life, but for years she remained sad, very sad all the time. It is said that she dreamed she was giving birth to a new son, named Mohammed. My father rejoiced in her dream and its beautiful interpretation, for it consoled the heart and soul of his beloved life companion during her time of grief and sorrow. Soon enough, the dream came true. She gave birth to a son, whom she named Mohammed bin Rashid Al Maktoum.

Every son can recall the love reflected in his mother's face. My mother was unique, tranquil and gentle.

My mother loved all her children deeply, but I always felt I was closest to her heart. I have never witnessed a love like hers, nor a heart like hers, nor a tenderness like hers. I spent my very first years within the warm embrace of my mother and father, my family. When I was two to three years old, my father would place me in front of him on his horse and take me with him wherever he went.

Every son can recall the love
reflected in his mother's face.
My mother was unique,
tranquil and gentle

I've always loved rising early. I used to get up before most others in the house, always to find my mother awake and preparing our breakfast, even though we had staff who could have done this for her.

I still remember the smell of my mother's bread and recall all our early morning conversations. I enjoyed our talks about herbal remedies, for she was well known for the medical skills she had mastered over the years. People travelled long distances with their children or relatives to have her prescribe herbal-based medicines and ointments for them.

My mother could also shoot better than many men; she could control a horse or camel better too, as if she had been born to be in the saddle. She met with other women and never hesitated to convey their concerns to Sheikh Rashid. She had a strong character but was enchanting at the same time. Everyone who knew her loved her deeply.

In the early 1960s

She would prepare my breakfast every day before I went to school. On my way, I would split the meal into two halves – one for me and the other for my beloved horse. I was young and thought bread with eggs was good for horses. My mother noticed that I was returning home from school very hungry. She learned that I was sharing my breakfast with my horse, so she doubled it. I thought this was simply a happy coincidence, until I realised as an adult that she had known all along.

This was my mother. She ate only after we ate. She rested only after we were asleep, and she rejoiced only after our grief had dissipated.

Regardless of the passing of days and nights,
your love remains always in my heart.
You are the brightest moon of all.
All my love and affection flows to you.

06

Latifa:
The Gift of Life

In my youth

Lamenting the death of his wife, Balqis, Nizar Qabbani wrote:

> Balqis...
>> Was the most beautiful of Babel queens
> Balqis...
>> Was the tallest of all Iraqi palm trees.
>> She gracefully walks
>> as if accompanied by peacocks,
>> and followed by oryxes.

These verses remind me of my mother when I was young. I remember her walking with a herd of deer, which she had cared for since her childhood. They accompanied her wherever she went. My mother was so beautiful, so elegant, with a queenly bearing that enchanted all around her.

The first time I gave my mother a gift, I was about seven years old. I was on a trip with Humaid bin Amhi, who was teaching me the art of hunting and desert survival skills. I saw a young fawn that had been abandoned by its mother. It is normal for a doe to leave the herd to give birth. Sometimes when the mother attempts to re-join the herd, she becomes frightened and leaves her fawn behind. Humaid's wife and I watched this happen. We waited until sunset approached, but the mother never returned.

I took the fawn up in my arms. In that moment, I knew who would replace its mother. I knew it would be my mother. She loved deer. My mother gave me life, so I would give this baby fawn the gift of life.

Her smile gave me life.
Her smile was the most
beautiful thing I had
ever seen!

My father came along with a group of men. After they gave Humaid the gifts my mother had sent, he took me and the fawn. I told them how I had discovered the abandoned animal and that I was going to give it to my mother.

I arrived home with the fawn still clutched close to me and when I saw my mother, I opened my arms, presenting her with the small deer. She was overjoyed and my heart nearly burst when I saw her happiness. When you surprise someone you love and they rejoice in it, your joy will be much greater, believe me!

Her smile gave me life. Her smile was the most beautiful thing I had ever seen!

There are many moments in life with my mother that I will never forget. I still remember sitting on her lap as she spoke to me about my very first trip to London. She told me about the strange country and great adventures that awaited me after I disembarked the huge flying machine that could cross oceans extending over miles and miles. I was astonished to learn that we would sleep in a tall building, in a country with a climate different to Dubai's where we slept on the roof on hot summer nights, sprinkling water down to cool us as it evaporated.

We never forget the wonder of our first eye-opening experience, our first discovery or the thrill of learning. I will never forget my mother's moving words.

I will never forget the sleepless night I had after my mother told me I would be visiting London for the very first time. It was back in 1959, the year after my father became Ruler of Dubai. My mother bought me an elegant jacket and two new *kanduras* (the long white robe, our national dress), I was happy, very happy! I was thrilled to own four *kanduras*. She suggested that I start wearing my two old ones when riding horses and camels, so she skilfully shortened them. Everything that made me happy, made her even happier.

Was there anyone else like you, mother?

07
Farewell to Latifa

At the funeral of my mother Sheikha Latifa bint Hamdan Al Nahyan in 1983

In May 1983, I lost my mother, Latifa bint Hamdan, the love of my heart. My father lost his life partner for over four decades. He lost his support, his darling, friend, companion and lover. My father lost my mother – the only person he wanted to prepare his breakfast every single day. He had grown accustomed to checking ongoing projects at daybreak, then coming back home to join her for breakfast and getting lost in conversation.

Who would prepare his breakfast now? Who would talk with him now? When she passed away, Rashid bin Saeed changed forever.

I, too, loved my mother and she loved me deeply. As any other child, I always claimed to be her favourite. A mother's greatness is reflected in her ability to make each of her children feel like they are the closest to her heart. When I grew up, I was always keen to make her happy. I was keen to bring back the perfect gift for her whenever I travelled abroad. Her happiness was my utmost pleasure. Her smile made my day every day, and her words, her words were the greatest comfort to me in this life.

Anyone who has never experienced a mother's love and affection has not fully experienced life. A mother's fatigue hurts us, a mother's grief breaks us into pieces and a mother's sickness exhausts us. We are afraid of even the smallest thing that might cause her pain. What if we lose her? What if she leaves us behind? A terrible pain, a great emptiness, a sense of abandonment – this is what we feel when we lose our mothers.

My father had regained his health and well-being after a period of illness only to be haunted by the trauma of loss. The strong, firm, steadfast victor who was never weakened or shattered, suffered greatly from the loss of his Latifa. He was never the same again.

I was so afraid for my father when my mother departed. We stayed at his side constantly in the wake of this shock that also distressed Dubai and its people, who sincerely loved the mother of Dubai.

Sheikha Latifa treated the sick, cared for the children, consoled the poor and listened to the women, sharing their joy and grief. I used to watch her supervise the preparation of food, which she would then share with her neighbours, relatives and guests.

I still remember the last time I saw her before she travelled to England to receive treatment. I kissed her. I hugged her. I held her tight. I took her hand in mine. She looked at me and said, "Is there anyone else like you?"

She expressed her admiration for the watch I was wearing on my wrist, and then she left. I started to think about the gift I would give her once she returned. I thought and thought, then decided to give her my watch. I felt as though she wanted part of me with her, to accompany her. I decided to give her the watch she liked.

Sadly, my mother never came back.

Her funeral was majestic. Thousands of people attended and many cried over the mother of Dubai. I lowered her into the grave as my father and brother watched me from above. I laid her down in her final resting place. Tears streamed down my cheeks.

A mother's fatigue hurts us,
a mother's grief breaks us into
pieces and a mother's sickness
exhausts us. What if we lose her?
What if she leaves us behind?

The funeral of Sheikha Latifa bint Hamdan Al Nahyan in 1983

> Our home changed
> after the loss of my mother.
> It changed forever. Nothing
> was the same now that all
> we had of her was a memory

As I was climbing out of her grave, my watch slipped off my wrist. Tongue-tied, I could not utter a word. I looked down at my watch next to her and felt a terrible pain. I thought, "Part of me with her, to accompany her."

Our home changed after the loss of my mother. It changed forever. Nothing was the same now that all we had of her was a memory.

After her death, my father was strong, noble and brave; patient, long-suffering and forbearing. After a few days, he invited Kamal Hamza, Head of Dubai Municipality, to visit us. Hamza came in a hurry in response to my father's invitation. My father asked his assistant, Salloum, to bring him a pen and a paper. His gaze reflected deep sadness but also pride. He said, "Write! I will dictate the will of our beloved deceased to you."

He burst into painful, bitter tears.

Hamza was surprised to see this happening. In front of other people, my father was the strong, stubborn knight; ever the amenable, capable leader. In public, my father was the engineer who brought Dubai to life; who built, who drove a renaissance, who led projects. My father won the admiration of the world.

No one ever expected to witness such a moment; the moment when this mighty warrior would collapse, to witness all this pain welling up inside him. They offered him a glass of water and reminded him of the mercy of God, until he finally calmed down. Soon after, he asked them to write down the will of his beloved deceased.

Once again, he burst into bitter tears, repeating: "The will of my beloved deceased, the will of my beloved deceased, the will of my beloved deceased."

08

In Search of 'Dubai' – A 185 Year Journey

Dubai Creek in the 1960s

Dubai was not founded by accident or coincidence. Rather, Dubai is the result of a journey that has endured more than 185 years. Dubai is the product of a long road of struggle and effort to overcome the dangers that have threatened its existence and longevity. I believe that Dubai is the pearl of the world and will forever remain so, God willing.

Dubai's journey began in the early 19th century, with Sheikh Maktoum bin Butti, the ruler who established our family's current legacy and laid the foundation for our modern way of life. His first and foremost objective was to make Dubai a safe place for all its inhabitants. He was succeeded by his brother, Sheikh Saeed bin Butti, who established absolute justice in the emerging emirate. The preservation of justice for all has been key to Dubai's longevity. It forms a central part of my family's legacy, as well as the first tenet of the emirate's unwritten constitution.

The reign of Sheikh Saeed endured through harsh years, during which wars between tribes and families broke out and spread. Sheikh Saeed firmly established internal security and fostered alliances with Abu Dhabi and the other emirates. He also succeeded in dealing with the British, negotiating a treaty that preserved our internal autonomy, while London oversaw all defence and foreign affairs. Balanced relations with all, as well as ongoing alliances, comprises the second tenet of Dubai's unwritten constitution.

Sheikh Hasher bin Maktoum took the reins in the second half of the 19th century for a 27 year period, during which Dubai benefitted from continued stability and economic growth. Sheikh Hasher was known for his wisdom and determination, and had great respect for the treaties that Dubai had with the British and neighbouring emirates.

In 1886, he was succeeded by Sheikh Rashid bin Maktoum, who ruled Dubai for eight years. During his reign, Sheikh Rashid promoted and enhanced the emirate's security and economic stability.

Then came Sheikh Maktoum bin Hasher, who assumed power in the late 19th century. He had an exceptionally brilliant economic vision, which enabled Dubai to achieve remarkable prosperity through trading and investment. In 1902, after the Iranian administration in Bandar Lengeh raised taxes for merchants on that side of the Gulf, Sheikh Maktoum abolished all customs duties on imports, opened up Dubai's port and welcomed all traders. As a result of adopting this free trade policy, goods flowed into and out of the city's port and in a short period Dubai became the Gulf's re-export hub. A significant number of major merchants trading in the Gulf area soon moved to Dubai and made it their regional headquarters. This was the third tenet of Dubai's unwritten constitution – to remain open to all, to adopt free trade principles and to welcome all who want to add value to our economy.

Following the death of Sheikh Maktoum in 1906, Sheikh Butti bin Suhail ruled Dubai for six years before he was succeeded by Sheikh Saeed bin Maktoum, my grandfather, in 1912. Under Sheikh Saeed's 46 year reign, Dubai's development propelled the emirate to an entirely new level and the heart of a modern city began to beat. Under his leadership, Dubai's population increased significantly, and its port welcomed an ever-increasing flow of maritime traffic carrying goods such as fabrics, herbs and incense. Sheikh Saeed continued to encourage free trade. Dubai's merchants operated unrestricted by fees, including tariffs and duties on pearl exports. Pearls constituted the largest trade sector in

> **66**
> The diversification of resources
> is a legacy passed down through
> my family. It is the guarantee
> that the lessons of our arduous
> journey over the past 185 years
> haven't been taken for granted
> **99**

the region until the collapse of the pearl market in the 1930s. That crisis cut off the lifeblood of the economy, but Dubai never stopped looking to its future and diversifying its trade. Our economic crisis deepened with World War II, but so did our determination to find alternative sources of trade and revenue.

In 1937, Sheikh Saeed signed an oil exploration agreement with Petroleum Development (Trucial Coast) Ltd. After 20 months of negotiations, an agreement granted the Iraq Petroleum Company exploration rights for 75 years in exchange for an annual fee of 30,000 rupees. Dubai had high hopes that oil would be discovered, especially when the company promised to pay 200,000 rupees to the Government of Dubai within two months of discovering commercial quantities of oil, as well as another three rupees for every barrel of oil that was exported. In the end, though, the company failed to find any of the precious resource.

Once again, Dubai had to pursue other sources of trade, revenue and opportunity. We continued to invest for the future and to focus on what we have always done best: trade in general, and servicing re-export markets in particular. Merchants would import goods from different markets to Dubai in large quantities at competitive prices and re-export them without incurring heavy taxation. Gold was the most important material being re-exported from Dubai, especially after World War II, when other countries blocked its import for

Downtown Dubai

economic reasons. Dubai's traders bought gold abroad, mostly through the United Kingdom, and sold the precious metal to traders supplying other markets in the region. The trade established Dubai, literally, as the 'City of Gold'. While gold continued to play a vital role during the 1950s and 1960s, it was not the only commodity being sold. Hundreds of other categories of goods were also shipped to the Gulf states, Iran, Iraq, the Indian subcontinent and East Africa.

My grandfather's legacy was to ensure economic diversification so that Dubai would never again rely on just one source of income. That principle was something my father, Sheikh Rashid, adopted through the construction of ports, the expansion of Dubai Creek, the development of free zones and the airport, as well as driving the launch of new economic opportunities, such as aluminium smelting.

People often ask me why Dubai is constantly launching new and different projects, including media zones, internet cities, technology accelerators, global ports and airports, as well as aviation, aluminium, real estate, advanced technologies, and Islamic and conventional banking companies, to name just a few. Why so much diversity?

Once again, the answer lies in Dubai's unwritten constitution. The diversification of resources constitutes the fourth pillar underpinning Dubai's success. It is a legacy passed down through my family. It is the guarantee that the lessons of our arduous journey over the past 185 years haven't been taken for granted. Free and open trade, economic diversification and entrepreneurialism are at the very heart of our city and its success.

09

The Great Storm – A Day of Judgement

The ship 'MV Dara' in 1961

When was the last time you did something for the first time? That question was posed by an Emirates airline advertisement, in which snow is falling outside the window of a hotel. Two travellers venture out: 'Enjoying the snow for the first time in their lives'.

When I saw the advert, it reminded me of childhood, when I used to witness little drifts of hail in the cold Dubai desert during our winter. I still remember, from the age of only ten years old, the talk of the elders who lived in the times of my grandfather, Sheikh Saeed. They would muse over the changes they had observed in the sea and the fishermen who returned with stories about unusual events. They spoke of strange fish from the deep showing up on the shore; of the spread of algae in areas it should not be found, and the sight of the seagulls massing before the storm. The elders talked about the Arabian bustard and the desert cottontail and how their habits were changing; about the winds – the force of which they had never experienced before; all signs that a powerful storm was about to strike Dubai. They likened these storms to the Day of Judgement but as I watched the calm blue sea, I didn't pay much heed to their prophetic, doom-laden words.

On the night of April 8th, 1961, I was sound asleep in my bedroom when I sensed a huge commotion, which left my heart pounding in my chest. I found my bed in the middle of a full-blown storm, with windows slamming in the gale-force winds that were blowing through our family home. My father shouted, "Hamdan... Mohammed... Your hands!"

I jumped and ran towards his voice. Hamdan called to me to bring my mattress to help shut the door. We all ran to him. My mother and sisters scrambled in search of any boards to shut the doors, preventing the wind from destroying everything. It seemed like the world was ending all around me, what some other cultures call the end of days. For us, it was the beginning of a seemingly endless night. People began to arrive in large groups at the palace in fear, asking for Sheikh Rashid's help. We could barely open the doors wide enough for them to enter due to the intensity of the winds that flattened anything standing in their way. It was a fearsome wind; the storm that the elders had warned us about. People arrived individually and in groups, bearing stories of pain and loss. I still remember my mother's face as she reassured a woman who was trembling with fear and unable to speak. My mother and sisters ripped up sheets to bandage the wounds of the injured who arrived on our doorstep. My father began to inquire about the extent of the damage in a low voice, so that fear would not spread throughout the house. With every answer, I could see the sadness and anguish on his face. There was heavy destruction, with palm trees flying through the air like toys, many houses damaged or utterly destroyed, and fishing boats tossed into the streets of the city. Many families suffered death or injury that night. My father did not wait to hear all the details. Within minutes, he divided the men into teams and gave them their instructions. The first group was to leave the palace to try to assess the damage at the hospital. My father said that medicine and medical supplies must be transported by any possible means and stored safely, as they would be needed very soon. There were many injured people at the hospital. Then arrived news that froze my father where he stood. British soldiers rushed past the door, scarcely catching their breath. They shouted, "Your Highness! There's a fire on the *Dara*!"

The world seemed to stand still. The *MV Dara* was a ship belonging to a British maritime company. It had operated for more than 13 years, transporting passengers and cargo from Mumbai and ports along the Gulf. When the storm broke, a strong explosion occurred in the ship's hold, causing a huge fire. More than 800 passengers were on board the sinking ship. The soldiers said that many were killed immediately, but more passengers were dying every minute as they crowded to escape – some crushed to death, others drowning in the raging waters. Overloaded lifeboats were capsizing in the middle of the sea and the strong winds were scattering the boats in all directions.

We gathered our relatives and a large number of Dubai residents in our home. My father sent all our family, without exception, with lifeboats to try to save anyone they could. We were able to rescue about 500 people that night – a night I thought would never end; one of horror, violence and terrible human tragedy. This state of upheaval continued for several days, during which my father did not sleep a wink. Although the winds had calmed, the aftermath of the storm hung over Dubai like a dark cloud for weeks. The toll of deaths and injuries was staggering. Every household had endured tragedy. Empty buildings were converted into makeshift homes and shelters. I learned never to underestimate the power of nature after that. I also learned the importance of being prepared at all times for an emergency. Despite the harshness of the storm, it showed the noble nature of the people of Dubai who came together in cooperation and support at a time of deep peril and distress. Despite the devastating losses, I learned how a leader must face a sudden crisis. The thing that marked me the most, and still does to this day, is that my father sent his own sons and nephews to save those drowning at sea before sending anyone else. Indeed, times of crisis reveal people's true colours.

10

The Kindest Man
I've Ever Known

Sheikh Saeed bin Maktoum and my father Sheikh Rashid bin Saeed Al Maktoum

One childhood memory I will never forget is the death of the kindest man I have ever known – my grandfather Sheikh Saeed bin Maktoum, may God have mercy on his soul.

No one could ever imagine Dubai without Sheikh Saeed, who spent 46 years ruling over the emirate, effectively launching it on its path to become a truly global city – a journey that it is my privilege to continue. My grandfather died on September 10th, 1958. I still remember that day, when his soul returned to its Creator just after the *Fajr* prayer.

My father had spent those last days by my grandfather's side, his grief was so great that during that time he barely ate. When the news broke, I clung to my mother's gown, as she struggled in vain to hold back her tears. The voices of women quietly mourning echoed through the space; they would not permit themselves to cry openly because this would seem like objecting to God's will.

Men gathered around my grandfather's house despite the stifling heat. They congregated in great numbers, overcome by silence, stillness and intolerable grief, while my father and some of his relatives went to perform the ritual washing of my grandfather. News of the death of Sheikh Saeed came as a bitter blow dealt to the people of Dubai. They loved him so, and appreciated his kindness, compassion and affection. He was an upright, caring, thoroughly decent man with an open and generous nature. As we say in Arabic, "Whatever he owned was for others."

He dealt with people with genuine concern, becoming a father figure to all. He never accepted unfairness and always sided with justice, even if it meant ruling against those closest to him. Sheikh Saeed was known for his magnanimity and for facing adversity with wisdom, tolerance and patience. Despite the many difficulties of his reign, my grandfather succeeded in establishing Dubai as a vibrant, thriving emirate and a significant commercial hub. During his reign, the pearl trade witnessed a great boom, boosted by Dubai's commercial and customs enablement. But what made Dubai the destination of choice for many pearl traders in those times was its distinctive society; it was always open and welcoming to others. It's no exaggeration to say that the seeds of the wide and peaceful cultural and social diversity we enjoy today were planted by Sheikh Saeed. Openness, tolerance and opportunities for all were some of the era's hallmarks. I am proud to say that they remain so today.

Under Sheikh Saeed's watch, Dubai went through many crises and each time, like the legendary phoenix, it would rise from the ashes stronger and more vibrant than ever.

With the Great Depression of the 1930s and the collapse of Dubai as one of the most important centres of the pearl trade, Sheikh Saeed found himself facing an unprecedented challenge. Dubai would endure even more tragedy as the century wore on. In February, 1939, a huge fire broke out in the Deira area, consuming some 300 houses and shops and claiming many lives. Dubai had scarcely turned the page on that painful chapter when an even greater disaster struck. Just a year later, in February 1940, another fire ravaged Bur Dubai, destroying more than 400 homes and shops. These and other disasters posed true tests of Sheikh Saeed's mettle. Time and again, he proved to be a leader with an indomitable will, displaying

Like the legendary phoenix, Dubai would rise from the ashes

unparalleled stability and presence of mind. Sheikh Saeed found not one but many alternatives to the pearl trade, and with his prescience and guidance, commercial activities in Dubai soon recovered. By the 1940s, the emirate reached a comfortable level of economic stability by diversifying its sources of income, improving services, developing its port and expanding land transport.

Sheikh Saeed's son, my honoured father Sheikh Rashid, also played a pivotal role in growing Dubai's economy. The young Crown Prince was Sheikh Saeed's right-hand man, never leaving his side throughout the various stages of Dubai's construction and reinvention. Dubai delivered on its promise of prosperity for its people and all those who came here in search of a better life.

In 1944, Dubai and several coastal emirates suffered a smallpox epidemic that destroyed many lives. Sheikh Saeed deployed all his resources to provide vaccinations for thousands of people. At that time, there was only a small dispensary barely able to meet the needs of our rapidly growing population, and a few clinics that did not provide comprehensive healthcare services. Sheikh Saeed decided to expand the dispensary and turn it into a hospital, which opened in 1951. This he did from his own private funds. He continued to develop and expand the facilities of the new Al Maktoum Hospital, spending on it generously, adding several new specialisms, hiring qualified medical personnel and providing the latest equipment and devices. It became one of the primary medical facilities in the region.

As for the education sector, Sheikh Saeed announced the establishment of the *Dar Al-Ma'aref* education board for Dubai in 1938, at a time when few would have understood its significance. With a healthy budget, it has been in charge of supervising education ever since. All this led to a quantum leap in educational services by the 1950s. It is said that one of the dearest things to Sheikh Saeed's heart was to see students early in the morning on their way to school. He would sometimes drive alongside them as they carried their school bags, waving out the window at them and welcoming the new school day together.

He was truly a great man; but death eventually claims us all, and I remember my grandfather's body being carried from the house, my father tightly gripping my hand as we walked behind the coffin in the funeral procession. I still do not know why he held me so tightly that day. Was it sadness, or did my father want me to remember that moment forever? What I do know, however, is that we will all make that final journey, no matter how long we live, how much we witness, how great our contribution. All that remains are the deeds a person has performed; they are what keeps their memory alive.

Good deeds raise a person's status before the Creator to Whom we all must return.

Many people, young and old, vied for the honour of carrying the coffin that held my grandfather's shrouded body. I looked back and saw my mother standing at the doorway in silence, while the women around her lamented. I walked beside my father as he held my hand.

I was still too small to see above the heads of the men in the procession, but in the spaces between I saw women standing in shop doorways weeping behind their *burqas*. The procession stopped at the house of Sheikh Saeed's eldest daughter, Sheikha Mozah bint Saeed, who loved my grandfather dearly and never left his bedside in those final, fateful days.

All too soon we arrived at the cemetery, three kilometres from the palace. My father and uncle slowly lowered the coffin that held my grandfather – the kindest man I have ever known – into the grave. I fought to hold back my tears. Then we prayed, giving thanks to God for the wonderful life Sheikh Saeed had graced us with.

While he was alive, my grandfather was the epicentre of my life; I spent most of my childhood with him. As I watched the crowds flowing to our house from every direction to offer their sympathy, I wondered what it all meant, knowing only that I would miss my grandfather.

Now my father would rule Dubai. The formal procedures and responsibilities began immediately; in fact, the men were already lining up to offer their condolences. I realised then that after the death of a ruler, his successor has no time to think about himself and his family. Time marches on, but responsibilities never stop.

11

Sheikh Rashid bin Saeed: A Visionary Ruler

With my father and brother Sheikh Hamdan bin Rashid Al Maktoum in 1963

The lessons of Sheikh Rashid bin Saeed know no end. He was an institution. He was an instructor. He was a ruler and, most importantly, he was a father to all.

His day started with the *Fajr* prayer and it was from him that I learned to wake and start every day in prayer.

He used to rise before dawn to pray, and then would begin his field trips immediately thereafter. He would go out to inspect all ongoing projects. Before breakfast, he would sit in front of the palace to receive officials, then go to his office near the Creek to meet with project supervisors. I enjoyed listening to him while he questioned them about the progress of various developments. They were always surprised to find that he knew more than they did about their work as he visited the sites every day at the break of dawn. Afterwards, he came back home to eat the breakfast my mother had made for him.

My father would not only meet with people once a day, during the so-called 'business hours'; he would always meet them again between *Asr* (mid-afternoon prayer) and *Maghrib* (sunset prayer).

My father's frequent visits to the developments across the city had three benefits. First, every project manager knew there was no opportunity for negligence or slacking. Second, the teams working on these projects knew they had Sheikh Rashid's attention and interest, which drove them to work harder and strive for more. Third, corruption and financial irregularity did not have a chance to thrive – every contractor and official knew they were under Sheikh Rashid's scrutiny. His visits served as a message to employees and a lesson to leaders and officials.

On the one hand, Sheikh Rashid was always keen to preserve Dubai's reputation and strove to settle all payments due to contractors and entrepreneurs on a swift, regular basis. He used to say that our real capital is our reputation with merchants. On the other hand, he never accepted any manipulation of applicable laws or regulations.

My father raised a horse, which he named Saqlawi. He fed him from a bottle, tamed him and trained him, all by himself. Saqlawi grew up loving Sheikh Rashid, and Sheikh Rashid loved Saqlawi in return. He used to ride his horse in the evening when he revisited development projects once again. At home, his horse would roam freely around the stable, ultimately reaching the palace door. My father taught Saqlawi to lift his front leg in the air to greet him when he raised his hand, and to bend on one knee when ordered. My father never tied Saqlawi up. He would ride out to a project site and dismount, leaving his horse untethered. Saqlawi followed my father as an obedient servant, then stood behind him as he talked to supervisors. I loved Saqlawi, for I realised that he had a similar personality to mine – and a sense of humour too!

Sheikh Rashid had an office alongside Dubai Creek. Through a mirrored glass window that overlooked the crane, he would watch the movement of ships, goods and commodities, as well as their loading practices. He knew all the ships and their owners. He even knew the volume of goods and commodities in place. When some new traders tried to evade paying customs duties by lodging complaints, Sheikh Rashid reminded them of their ships and prosperous business, explaining to them that the government had the right to claim its share. Merchants were always surprised by

Sheikh Rashid's knowledge of their trade activities across the Creek, for which they showed him great respect and appreciation.

From the very beginning, my father focused on developing the Creek. To him, the most important objective was to expand, deepen and open the waterway to receive larger ships. To that end, Sheikh Rashid ordered the Creek dredged. The scooped out rock and sand was used to restore areas regularly flooded by the tides. This land was then sold to pay for the cost of the works. As a result, the Creek became deeper and attracted more and bigger ships, further contributing to the promotion of trade in Dubai. From that moment on, I inherited my father's passion for projects that enhance the city.

My father's reign was characterised by the abundance of projects he set in motion, including the launch of Dubai Creek and Dubai International Airport, as well as of telecommunications, water and electricity companies. Additionally, he oversaw improvements made to Al Maktoum Hospital and other investments in social development. Whether in government or business, this is my idea of a leader – a person who progresses, creates, builds and serves others.

From a very early age, I learned that the leader is the most capable person to implement projects efficiently. I also learned that every dirham is valuable and should be spent very carefully. The culture of governance established by Sheikh Rashid bin Saeed is based on the principles of wise spending and refraining from wasteful practices in government. One of the key secrets to Dubai's success is the governance values established by Sheikh Rashid; values that now define the country and are shared by all its people.

12
Lessons in Leadership

With my father Sheikh Rashid bin Saeed Al Maktoum

My father began his rule in 1958 with great energy, eager enthusiasm and high spirits. Every day I watched him in action taught me a new lesson, bringing me fresh ideas, exciting projects and eventually greater understanding, perhaps even a little wisdom.

One of the very first decisions Sheikh Rashid made was to establish dedicated councils for traders, merchants and any other skilled people in our society, such as builders, engineers and intellectuals. When I asked him why he had invited all these new figures to share their views, he looked at me seriously and said, "A man does not stop learning. We want them to help us build Dubai. We want them to teach you how to be a leader. This is the start of your training."

That was the very first simple but profound lesson I learned from Sheikh Rashid: that no man is born perfect; we all need the minds and souls of others to complete our own. Everyone must continue learning no matter how much he or she achieves. A leader needs the counsel of others to learn more, and to win their support for new plans and projects. Only an ignorant person turns a blind eye to advice.

At an early age I learned that even the Prophet Muhammad – may the peace and blessings of God be upon him – was not afraid to consult his companions. Later, I learned that one of the most difficult challenges a ruler can encounter is knowing when to heed honest advice and inconvenient truths. I grew up and watched Arab rulers and governments who never listened to their people, who ignored their citizens' dreams, hopes and aspirations. I saw leaders of great nations overthrown because they made fundamental mistakes: they listened only to their most sycophantic advisors; surrounding themselves with people who glorified, praised and complimented their every action.

The age-old tale of *The Emperor's New Clothes* still applies to many leaders today; they are so blinded by pride and flattery that they cannot see the naked truth. The worst thing a leader or ruler can do is to choose bad counsel. I grew up in the realisation that Sheikh Rashid's principles are timeless. His advice is still valid today and will continue to be relevant forever.

On another day, in another council, I learned a great lesson that I still apply. Sheikh Rashid told one of the council's members that he believed him to be an efficient man with leadership capabilities. He asked him if he could launch a project and follow up on its completion until the very end? Later, I whispered to him that I did not think the man was that efficient or deserved such praise. Sheikh Rashid responded that one of the most important qualities of a successful ruler is to surround him or herself with strong leaders. We should always be on the lookout for them. We should also be the ones nurturing them. It is our duty to create leaders, to develop their talents, give them responsibility and encourage them to become genuine leaders. Those were priceless words of wisdom that reflect the essential secret of a nation's success and excellence: that the creation of leaders is the main enabler of development and further progress. As with nations, so with business and also with your own family. The worst thing you can do is be the one and only leader. This was the second lesson I learned from Sheikh Rashid. I have applied this principle for more than half a century in my own career. I launched dedicated programmes to prepare and create leaders. I took great care to invest in the ambitious young people who surrounded me throughout the various stages of my career. Today, I see them becoming world-class leaders in their own areas of specialisation.

One of the most important
qualities of a successful ruler is
to surround him or herself with
strong leaders

I attended public events with my father

Sheikh Rashid preferred to stay away from the babble of politics and its messy entanglements

I am very proud of them – all of them. Taking advice to heart expands your mind, and the creation of leaders multiplies your own efforts. The leaders we create are the eyes through which we see, the hands with which we build and the creative energy we add to our own to realise our vision.

The third lesson I learned from Sheikh Rashid came when I was young and I asked him who the real leaders are in this world. He replied that today's real leaders are not the same as yesterday's. Today's leaders are the silent giants who possess the money, not the politicians who make the noise. This answer still amazes me, for I see it borne out in truth every day in our modern world. Economics always drives politics, and not just in Western countries and major democracies. Today, I look at a big country like China that challenges the whole world, establishing geopolitical reach and influence, gathering and building international alliances, less due to its military power (which is considerable) but more because of the power of its economy. It is starting to rival the United States, still the world's leading superpower, not only because of its overwhelming military strength but also because of its unparalleled economic and cultural influence. This answer summarises much of

I was rarely far from my father's side

Dubai's current thought and philosophy, and encapsulates Sheikh Rashid's political positions and beliefs. He preferred to stay away from the babble of politics and its messy entanglements as it is of little benefit to us in the Arab world. Rather, Sheikh Rashid's concentration, energy and time was focused on development projects and the economy, avoiding any overt confrontation that could drag our country into a political quagmire. I believed in and adopted this philosophy and advice with conviction and faith, as well as experience, throughout my long career. Today, many Arabs see our country's development as the most successful in the region. In annual surveys, thousands of young Arabs report that they wish their countries would follow our nation's model – a true beacon of hope. Many aspire to move to the UAE so they can achieve their dreams and realise their ambitions. Today, Dubai has become a global economic icon, thanks to the principles Sheikh Rashid instilled in us and made part of our national culture. These are the three lessons passed to me from a wise man and a tutor who helped shape my life and career. It is sound advice that guides my pursuit of the happiness and well-being of my people.

13

My Little Cave

Many people have a 'cave' of their own to which they retreat to practise their hobbies, stay away from the hubbub of the house or relax after the stress of a long day's work.

The desire to have my own quiet retreat grew inside of me when I was young. We had a small, sandy room, located in the west wing of the Zabeel Palace. My father kept his hunting falcons in this room. When he was occupied with development projects, leaving him little time for sport, he asked me to take care of this room. I did, but in my own way.

I remember he came to see me one afternoon. I was sitting on the sandy ground in the small room, looking proudly at my new paradise and thinking about how I would like my father to see it, when the door opened. I turned to see his serious face and features, soon lit up by a grin and accompanied by a booming laugh, as he called out to my mother.

The room had turned from a hunting falcons' roost into a small zoo, crammed with the various animals that I had caught. There were many scorpions. Boxes, filled with snakes of all species, were stacked on top of each other. What little space remained was filled with shells and fish skeletons that I collected during my trips to the beach and carried gently to the room.

My father and mother stood at the entrance and laughed. They laughed so hard that I could not understand what they were trying to say. When my mother managed to take possession of herself, she wiped her laughing tears, saying, "Oh, so it was no mere thief that stole the jars from my kitchen then! Could you at least give me my *oud* perfume box back, sweetheart? This *oud* is worth much more than the feathers of those birds you keep in there!"

After that, this room became the first place to be searched when any jar in the house went missing. In response to my disappointment at having to give up some of my precious tools, my father and mother decided to enrich my scientific investigations. My mother gave me notebooks, in which I started to write down my discoveries about the birds, animals, shells and skeletons I had collected.

Those books were filled with my notes, observations and drawings. They were my educational pleasure and that room was my little 'cave', where I furthered my knowledge about nature and collected its various small creatures.

I learned a lot from this little cave, from observing all these little lives so closely. I learned that study and exploration teach you lessons that stay with you throughout your life.

14

My First Horse

What is the difference between your first love and your first horse? To me, there is no difference, no difference at all. To me, a first love and a first horse are two sides of the same coin.

I have loved horses since I was a child. I was raised in a time and place where it was natural for my father to roam around Dubai on the back of his horse, Saqlawi, with no bridle or reins. My older brother Maktoum had an especially close bond with his horse. If someone else tried to ride that horse it would buck and throw them off. Maktoum's horse was never able to tolerate anyone but him – may his soul rest in peace. I remember Hamdan's horse, Karawan, named after the curlew for its speed. How could I not love horses when I grew up with a mother who could ride one bareback?

I grew up as part of a family in which horses were loved, where our parents would gather us round the fire in winter and tell us myths and tales about these marvellous creatures. In one of these stories, it was said that when God wanted to create the horse, He told the South Wind, "I am the Creator, and from you I shall create. I shall make a proud creation for my people and their descendants, which will be a thing of beauty for them, a humiliation to their enemies, and a protector of those who obey me."

The Wind told Him to perform as He wished, and thus the Lord composed a mare and pronounced her an Arabian, whose goodness is shown on her forelock, who carries fortune wherever she goes and who He gave the power to fly without wings.

We inherited this love for horses, and I always feel their greatness when I am in their presence. The elder women used to say that no evil

From my horse, I learned
that unconditional love is
returned, that patience and
dedication are rewarded
and that giving your all to
achieve success is the only
path to victory

spirit would dare to enter a tent in which an Arabian horse dwells. This is the environment in which I was raised and grew up, so how could I not love horses?

In the Holy Quran, God the Almighty said, "By the steeds that run, with panting breath", and the Prophet (PBUH) affirmed, "Goodness is tied to the forelocks of horses until the Day of Resurrection".

Hence, only an honourable man would honour a horse. That being said, again, how could I not love horses?

Today, it is said that I am one of the leading horse owners in the world. What many do not know is that in my childhood, when my mother would look for me and not find me in my bed at night, she knew that she might find me in the stable, sleeping on the straw. I loved my horse deeply. I understood my horse and she understood me. If I left, she asked about me. If I was near her, I talked to her and she talked to me.

> The love of charging horses surges in my blood.
> > I love even the mention of their name.
> Those who don't appreciate them,
> > as those ignorant of falcons would roast them.
> The flashing hooves of fighting horses
> > spark fire and kindle flame.
> I have cared for them all of my life,
> > I love them, I can't be without them.
> If my horses miss me they go out looking for me.
> > They can find me just by the scent of my clothes.
> I have given them what I've lived of my life,
> > and I will gift them the remainder.

My relationship with horse racing started on a beautiful evening when I was coming back home from the desert with my father. Riding, he told me, "I want to organise a horse race in Dubai. The race will be open to all tribes and I want you to take part."

I was about ten years old, but the sentence my father uttered made me feel like I was 20 or 30 years old. My father's words energised me and granted me an even greater responsibility, for the race would constitute a major celebration everyone would witness, a major celebration in which everyone would participate and compete.

> ❝
>
> I loved my horse deeply.
> I understood my horse and
> she understood me. If I left,
> she asked about me. If I was
> near her, I talked to her
> and she talked to me
>
> ❞

My father owned a string of horses. He said, "Pick one and train it in preparation for the race."

Of course, I was the third to choose a horse, as I was the third among my siblings. My brother Maktoum, took the lead, followed by Hamdan, and then I chose third, for an older brother's respect should always be assumed in all cases. This is how we were raised. This is what we grew up learning. To this day, I personally cannot understand anyone who does not respect their elders.

I noticed a beautiful, yet injured, pony that had never been raced before. I watched her carefully and realised that she could race easily. She was named Sawda Umm Halaj – the black one with the earring.

It was known that when the Arabs preferred a horse over any other, they would adorn its ear with a gold earring, and some would also put gold and silver necklaces to adorn the neck of their favourite horse, just as a beautiful woman does.

Sawda's earring had caught at some time and torn her ear leading to her name – Umm Halaj. Straight away I started preparing to train Sawda, and the first step was treating her injured leg. My mother, Latifa, knew best about herbal remedies, and about horses as well. I asked her to check my pony as I was worried about her injury.

My mother examined her carefully. From the very beginning, I noticed the pony's interaction with my mother as she started to examine her limbs and joints, trying to determine the cause of her pain. The pony knew that my mother was there to treat her. This is when I first realised the pony's intelligence, sensitivity, tenderness and loyalty.

My mother located the injury on her leg and asked me to trim Sawda's hooves, put a herbal poultice on the injury and give her a herbal syrup to relieve pain. My mother asked me to start training her gently and walk her gradually, changing her dressing daily. That was the most important project of my young life! The race was set to begin in four months and I needed three months to treat and train my horse. I still remember the medicine, as I was keen to prepare and apply it to her leg daily all by myself. My mother's treatment was a mixture of *harmel* (rue), turmeric and *Sidr* honey, as well as other beneficial ingredients. This mixture made a poultice, which was replaced daily.

I started to spend more time in the stables, and the swelling started to fade as I fed her doses of turmeric for ten days. The limb appeared cleaner under the bandage, however, the ligament still looked unpleasant, so I made sure to keep on applying the poultice. I also made sure to rest her, walk her daily and increase the exercise as her lame leg improved.

By the end of the third month, she was walking four to five hours a day. She would always have an ungainly looking tendon, but a strong, ugly looking tendon is better than a beautiful, weak one.

It was a good distance between Zabeel Palace and the sea. I used to leave the house in the morning and spend the day on the long, white stretch of sand. My horse and I would train on the beach, swimming into the sea to cool off. We would have lunch with friends and I would feed her the fresh desert grass I had picked for her. Every now and then she would put her head up when her mouth was full, chewing the food. She put her injured leg forward when she ate, like a ballerina.

When it was time to leave, I would whistle to her and she followed me happily back to the stables. She enjoyed it as much as she did our outings. She would stand calmly, her sleepy eyes soft and shining, while I brushed the sand and salt from her coat. She would flick her ears back and forth, following the intonation of my voice as I talked to her the whole time. Then she used to put her injured foot forward as if reminding me of her pain. Once I finished applying the poultice, I would try to find something else to do; any excuse not to leave the stables. I wanted to be beside her all the time.

> ❝
> From this beautiful horse,
> I learned so much. I learned how
> to establish a true relationship
> with this remarkable species
> — a relationship of loyalty
> and friendship
> ❞

From this beautiful horse, I learned so much. I learned how to establish a true relationship with this remarkable species — a relationship of loyalty and friendship. I learned how to talk to horses and how to understand them. I learned that goodness can flourish and evolve into greatness when invested in raising horses. From this beautiful horse, I learned the true meaning of loyalty.

From my first horse, I learned that achievements are never accomplished without work. I spent three long months treating my horse, cleaning her wound, changing her bandages and making her walk for hours every day, spending together the best of times at the beach.

From my horse, I learned that unconditional love is returned, that patience and dedication are rewarded and that giving your all to achieve success is the only path to victory.

15

My First Race

My first race on my first horse! This was an occasion to be remembered for a lifetime and, indeed, I still recall it as if it were yesterday. These brilliant moments of youth stay engraved forever in your heart and soul. They never fade.

The news of the race my father had announced spread far and wide. Maktoum trained Oudeh, a descendent of the Widthen family, while Hamdan prepared Hamdaniah for the race. I was happy with Sawda Umm Halaj, very happy!

Crowds of people from all of the emirates came to watch and participate in the race. My family, as well as the people of Dubai, felt that this was a public invitation, so each house and family decided to cook for the tribes coming to attend the event. Animals were gathered and slaughtered in preparation for such an occasion. Weeks before the race, women prepared perfumes for the guests to wear and enjoy following the feast. Poets composed and practised performances to recite in public, especially for the event. The men bragged about their horses and each claimed his was the greatest.

Riding alongside my brother Sheikh Hamdan bin Rashid Al Maktoum

My father ordered a two-kilometre track be prepared along Jumeirah Beach. Competitors came from neighbouring emirates, set up their tents and camped with their horses. Banners were put up at the start and finish lines. The atmosphere was electric, the crowds buzzed with anticipation.

I arrived there the day before the race. My older brothers Maktoum and Hamdan sent me ahead to set up camp for the three of us. That night I walked the two-kilometre strip with my mare on a lead rope, telling her of the great race to come. Tomorrow would be our chance to prove ourselves to my father and all his friends. During our walk, I noticed that the track was good in the centre, but the sand had piled up and formed mounds like tiny dunes at the edges. It would not be to one's advantage to leave the middle of the track, that was for sure.

The morning of the race dawned after a restless night of dreams and anticipation. I woke up and blinked the sleep out of my eyes. Then I blinked again thinking that perhaps it had blurred my vision, but it had not. A thick blanket of mist lay over Jumeirah Beach. The Sheikhs and competitors had gathered over coffee and dates to discuss the weather. I hurriedly put on the old *kandura* I had cut short and rushed to my mare; there was the poultice to wash off and breakfast to feed her before I could go and listen to the news. I finished and then ran to sit at my father's feet, where one of his friends handed me some bread and coffee.

The race was on! It was not dangerous fog, they had decided. You could still see 50 metres in front of you. My nerves jangled and my stomach turned somersaults.

> My first race on my first horse!
> These brilliant moments of youth
> stay engraved forever in your
> heart and soul. They never fade

I went to get my mare and walk her before the race. Her muscles rippled under her midnight-black coat. I had combed her mane down with water so it lay long, with the ends singed red by the sun. Other horses were also walking with their riders, and she seemed to be sizing them up just as I was.

Maktoum had trained Oudeh but he had asked Saluma Al Amri to ride his mare. He himself had nearly always ridden in these races, but today the stakes were high and he had chosen Saluma for his weight. There were others – many others – but I was sure it was Oudeh we would have to beat.

Finally, they ordered us to mount and we all made our way to the start. The starter stood there with his pistol raised above his head and *kandura* flapping in the wind. I fixed my eyes on his hand, trying to make out the muscles in his finger that would pull the trigger. I spoke to Umm Halaj softly and in my peripheral vision I could see her one torn ear flicker back and forward in response. I ran my fingers through her thick mane.

Suddenly, a loud crack ripped through the morning mist and a huge cheer erupted down the beach. We were off!

My breath caught in my throat and I gasped in wonder as Umm Halaj charged powerfully forward. I made sure to hold tight as I was riding her bareback. All around me, horses surged ahead like a great tidal wave, and shouts from the jockeys and whoops from the onlookers filled the air. It did not take more than a furlong for the field to settle into what looked like a pattern, and out ahead of me I saw Saluma with Oudeh disappearing like a ghost into the mist. He must have been looking for an early lead, meaning to use the fog as a blanket.

I decided not to wait with the others and save my horse but to stalk him. Saluma was experienced enough to know how much he could push Maktoum's mare and I could not afford to let him out of my sight. I urged Umm Halaj on with my legs and she leapt forward to chase after him. My heart swelled with pride. What could be more wonderful than to ask a horse and feel them give you all they had?

Saluma had what must have been a five-length lead. Just as the mist had helped him create it, now it helped me to creep up slowly behind him. He must have felt something from his mare, for the sound of hooves and cheering, accompanied by the crashing waves of the sea, would have drowned out anything else. He looked behind to see me clinging to Umm Halaj, whose head was now near Oudeh's flank. The look on his face was one of such surprise I had to bite down hard on my tongue not to let out a peal of laughter. He was favouring the middle to the right side of the track; I had two horses' width between me and the deeper sand.

I was waiting for the flag to appear in the mist when I saw him push harder. Had he seen the flag before me? I looked up in confusion and tried to make it out; it should be near now. Then he made his move. Seeing me try to come up from the inside, he gently began to drift me towards the deep sand. I caught sight of the flag. There was no time to go around him; I could only struggle forward.

I asked Umm Halaj for all she had, and she definitely gave it to me. Floundering in the deeper sand, she made up the two lengths he had gained on us. My heart was in my mouth as I drew up alongside him, but in the final bobbing of heads, Oudeh beat us by one. Hamdan came flying in behind me for third place.

What a win for my father's stables! We dominated the results and I felt like a king as my two older brothers ran to pat me on the back, and my father's friends walked around Umm Halaj and regarded her critically as I cooled her down. I patted her until my hand tingled. My father walked up and smiled, "Well done, Mohammed. Well done."

If only this moment could last forever! That evening was magical. The air was full of energy and happiness. Flames reached for the skies and mesmerised the men who sat talking. That evening during the festivities, Maktoum, Hamdan and I all sat together at the fireside. We decided that my mare had proved herself beyond all doubt. By the campfires, the men said that experience was what beat her.

They said she would have streaked past Oudeh had I not been caught in the deep sand. They were right, we all knew. Nobody blamed me;

My breath caught in my throat and I gasped in wonder as Umm Halaj charged powerfully forward

everyone was proud of my first race. I felt a tinge of regret at my lack of experience, but nothing could take away from the swell of pride I felt in my chest when Hamdan said he would add Umm Halaj to his own string. Who could have imagined that the older brother I revered would want a mare I had trained?

That night when my brothers slept, I rose and walked over to my mare. Laying with her legs gathered to herself in the sand, she raised her head and whickered a quiet greeting as I approached. I stood in front of her and traced the shape of the white star that lengthened into a thin strip on her black face. I let my fingers follow the whirl of hairs in the middle of her forehead. She sighed deeply. I bent to kiss her on her torn ear and then sat down.

I told her that she would be going to Hamdan now. That is the way of the desert; filial duty is paramount. It was an honour that he wanted

My brother Sheikh Maktoum bin Rashid with Sawda Umm Halaj

her, but it nevertheless made my heart feel as though it had been punctured in my chest.

Hamdan had said that I could choose another horse from him. After a few days, I had been watching one of his horses. She had been raced before, but she had one or two problems similar to Umm Halaj. I waited until I saw that Hamdan was in a good mood and then I asked him for her. He smiled and led her to me. Her name was Rumanieh. We were back in business!

16

At Last!
An Airport
in Dubai

Dubai International Airport in the 1960s

My first trip to London in the summer of 1959 with my father was a turning point in my youth. I loved London even before reaching it. My mother told me of the fantastic adventure this trip would be, to a land of endless greenery and tree-lined streets and avenues. It was cool enough that people would sleep indoors, rather than on the roof as we did in Dubai. She told me of the thronging crowds, of how differently the people dressed and that there were great horse races held on grass.

My father, however, had another perspective. He had spent the few days before the trip in silence. He was thinking about how he would address the important topics to be discussed with the Macmillan Government and how he could return from London with the maximum gain. Our feelings towards the British were cool but courteous. At the very heart of the matter was the reality that we were waiting for the day they would leave our country. Our relationship was governed by treaties and conventions, under which we controlled our internal affairs, while they assumed responsibility for our foreign relations and defence.

My father's silence was interrupted by my many questions about who we were going to meet. He told me we will meet the Prime Minister and explained that the Prime Minister had the authority of a Sheikh. "But what then is the role of the Queen?" I asked.

"She also has the authority of a Sheikha, but the Prime Minister is the most important one there," he replied.

I asked what we will discuss and he responded, "Mohammed, I want you to concentrate on the discussions and listen carefully to all that

The impossible is a choice, and the world opens doors to those who know what they really want!

the translator says. We will discuss many important topics. We want an airport in Dubai," he said. I agreed with him dutifully.

For years, the aircraft coming into Dubai had mainly been Imperial Airways and BOAC flying boats, which landed on the Creek. By the 1950s, the seaplanes had been replaced by airliners, yet we still had no facilities to handle commercial traffic, which used to fly into Sharjah airport. My father wanted to build a commercial runway for Dubai but the British refused, saying Sharjah's airport was sufficient and protected by their military base. They saw it as a security issue while we saw it as a developmental one – travel to us back then was a tedious affair involving many stops along the way. The trip to London was crucial to resolving this issue.

I stood behind my father as the door of the plane opened, and before I could see beyond my father's towering form, England greeted me with a rush of cool crisp air. London's airport looked like an ant colony! People were rushing to catch flights and queuing to enter

The first airfield at Dubai International Airport in 1959

and leave. The airport itself was both amazing and frightening, a symbol of the powerful economy that drove it. It was enough to make you respect the country behind it. An airport is the first face of a country that any visitor encounters. It reflects the power, economy and status of a country. It also reflects the wish of millions of people to visit the city. Would there ever become a day when our airport could be like London's? It was a dream that would assume reality through the years. At the time, I had no clue what the future held for me and for Dubai. I knew, though, one thing for sure; that we are no less than others.

We shook hands with many people before we climbed into the waiting cars. Maktoum, who had accompanied us, constantly had to stop and push me forwards, otherwise I would have been left standing in amazement at the place. As we pulled away, I sat with my nose glued to the window. My mother was right about all the green! Nothing could have prepared me for the beauty of this land. There were green hills that rolled away like waves on the sea. There were fields; large squares of brilliant yellow mustard plant flowers. And the birds; the birds were glorious! I broke my reverie just long enough to beg my father to have them drive slower so I could see these birds. He smiled, telling me there would be time for that later and we rushed on to the hotel.

When we arrived to our room, my father sat on the end of the bed, seemingly engulfed in deep thought. I woke up early in the morning, as the sounds of sirens through the night gave me a restless sleep. I opened my eyes to see my father's smile. "Wonder makes a young man tired, Mohammed. Come; wash, pray and dress. We must go to meet the Prime Minister."

When we arrived at Downing Street, I was seated opposite their 'Sheikh Macmillan Prime Minister', as I would call him. I remembered to sit up and listen as my father had told me. My father sat to Macmillan's right. I was studying this leader intently when I became alarmed. I saw him start to cross his legs. It was a great insult in the Arab world to cross your legs so that the sole of your shoe faces your guest. I was about to react when he crossed his legs away from my father. I breathed a long sigh of relief, loud enough that my father read my thoughts and shot me a stern but encouraging smile.

As they discussed the airstrip, I listened intently to the translator who was very polite as he relayed my father's forceful words. His argument was passionate, that Dubai needed this runway for its development and to connect it to the world. At the end of the discussion, we got what we had travelled there for: permission to develop the runway.

Dubai International Airport in the 1950s

Indeed, in the 1970s, years after the new airstrip was first built in Dubai, my father commissioned me to lead the development efforts at the airport. I added new terminals and facilities to increase capacity and announced the adoption of an open skies policy. I linked such efforts with the development of tourism by launching Dubai's first tourism strategy. We later founded the Emirates airline, and invested massively to develop Dubai International Airport as a global hub.

Today our airport is the busiest international airport in the world. Our city welcomes more than 20 million tourists each year, and in excess of 113 airlines connect us with the world. The impossible is a choice, and the world opens doors to those who know what they really want!

17

Diving for
a Living

My father asked me to add a new skill to my repertoire, something that would expose me to an aspect of life I wasn't used to seeing. He wanted me to learn about the sea by going on pearl diving voyages. Dubai's once-great pearling fleet was reduced to just a few boats, but a few men still made a living from fishing and diving back then.

I was already used to swimming in the shallow sea with friends. What stood out in my memory was that the sea had its own special smells and sounds. Its aroma is strong, filling the lungs and energising the spirit, like the smell of grass when it rains after a dry spell. And oh, how beautiful is the sound of the sea; raging waves or calm ones, bringing comfort to the soul and sparking creativity in the heart, especially when the reverberations of the waves mix with the calls of the gulls circling above the fishing nets, as if they were expressing their joy over the abundant catch. These were my impressions of the sea: sounds, smells and happy memories of playing with friends or on horseback on its beautiful shore. What I did not know was that the sea was more than sounds, smells and childhood memories: it also represented the joys, sorrows, hopes, pain and stories of all Dubai's seafaring people; stories I could not imagine until my father asked me to take to the sea.

My father would sometimes send me to a man named Abu Jaber, one of the heads of the fleet, who had worked his way up to this position through accumulated experience and inherited knowledge. His nickname was *Sardal*, which in the language of seafaring folk is the most experienced person with the most knowledge of the sea, the winds and the tides. It is the *sardal* who announces the beginning of the diving season, waiting for the calm sea of summer before doing so, and it is he who declares its end at the beginning of winter.

The *sardal* announces the beginning of the season based on the movement of the waves. He knows directions by tracking the positions of the stars. The *sardal* has the capacity to map the local waters and all they contain in his mind. Just as we can read the desert land from footprints and imagine what events have taken place there, we can use those same principles to visualise the seabed and study its nature. Sailors used to tie a heavy mass of lead onto a rope and throw it into the sea to determine the depth of the water. They measured the distance in arm spans. Abu Jaber could tell what was at the bottom of the sea by looking at what clung to the lead mass, and he could measure the strength of the waves by feeling the movement of the rope.

The people of Dubai used to dive mainly in the summer. For those unfamiliar with summer in Dubai, the deep waters are comfortably warm during this season, allowing the diver to descend repeatedly to collect oysters containing precious pearls. At the surface, however, the heat is scorching, causing many sailors to become dehydrated. One truly marvellous discovery that can be made on diving trips is fresh water springs and streams in specific areas of the sea, which allow divers and sailors to drink their fill. Only experienced seamen knew where to find these sites.

There was also 'cold diving' or 'winter diving', for those who had not enjoyed much luck during the blazing hot summer months, forcing them to try their hand again in the winter. Cold diving was more difficult because the low temperatures forced divers to shorten the time they spent below the surface. The often unstable seas, with choppy waves and violent winds, posed great dangers for small

A leader must be on the ground living among the people, enduring their conditions and experiencing their lives

diving boats. How many bad tidings did those winds carry to the people of Dubai?

My father sent me to Abu Jaber to learn about the sea, its conditions, its riches and its seasons. But the most important thing I learned from my journeys was how difficult life at sea could be, and the many challenges our people faced when seeking their livelihood from its bounty. The people of Dubai were accustomed to the hardship of living not only in the desert but also at sea. One can only understand this by living with them and going out for fishing and diving trips as one of them.

Some say a leader must have a bird's-eye view, looking at things from above so that he or she can assess them and make the relevant decisions. I say a leader must be on the ground living among the people, enduring their conditions, experiencing their lives and knowing the minute details of their suffering in order to change their situation for the better.

I always experienced deep feelings of awe and respect as I watched the divers get ready for their perilous journeys down to the seabed. During these trips, I helped with the preparation process, such as loading supplies onto the boats, usually some dates, dried meats and water. The *sardal* would locate the areas that contained pearls. The diver would jump into the water, placing a fish bone on his nose to close it, and a rope around his body, held by the *sayeb* – the person who would pull him up. The diver would fill his lungs with air and submerge. No one on board would utter a word. All you could hear was the sound of the boat bobbing in the waves. The instant the diver tugged on the rope, the *sayeb* would quickly pull him up. He would emerge breathless, lacking even the energy to swim to the water's surface.

It is not surprising that so many accidents and fatalities occurred while pearl diving.

The sailors would recite the funeral prayer for the deceased and then slip them back into the sea. Sometimes, divers would drown as a result of the *sayeb*'s negligence or his failure to feel the tug of the rope. Other times, when divers were lifted back onto the boat, they would not be able to breathe properly and would asphyxiate. The lucky ones would return with only minor injuries, such as a popped eardrum. In those cases, a piece of iron would be heated and placed on the eardrum to speed the healing, causing the victim to endure severe pain and scream in anguish.

Despite the tragedies, these journeys also had a wonderful side to them; there was the hard work, the spirit of cooperation among the crew, the great exuberance and pride of the pearl harvest, and lovely evenings full of stories of adventures and wonderment. The return from these voyages was a major social event, with an army of joyous children and women coming out to welcome their families; a festive chorus mixed with the sounds of paddles and the breaking of the waves on the beach.

I learned that the sea was not only sounds and smells, but the spirit of perseverance, the human stories and the feelings of joy or despair it sparked in the hearts of so many.

I remember taking a quiet moment to sit and contemplate the sea, passing my fingers through the white sand and praying to God to help me serve these people one day.

18

Maktoum – More Than A Brother

With my brother Sheikh Maktoum bin Rashid Al Maktoum in 1961

I was awakened from a sound sleep by a hand gently shaking my shoulder. "Mohammed, Mohammed, wake up! It is me, Maktoum," my elder brother said. He quickly took a few steps back, for he knew that my first response would be to jump out of bed, ready to fight!

He smiled a little and said, "Hold on, Mohammed! It is me, Maktoum!" He was holding a flashlight that added a touch of warmth to his face amid the room's cold air. "My mare will give birth soon. You asked me to wake you," he whispered. A big smile stretched across my face as I immediately rushed to wash and follow him towards the stables.

His eyes were wide and tender, the same as my mother's. His cheeks were full and his face was adorned with two moles: one on his left cheek and another on his chin. He was the kindest, softest, humblest and most considerate among us all. He was quite different. My mother used to say, "He bears a resemblance to your grandfather, Sheikh Saeed – may God have mercy on his soul."

Maktoum loved horses dearly, and he knew the signs when a mare was about to foal, as his intuition never failed him. This is why I asked him to wake me up when the birth of his horse approached. I looked up to him as my idol and hero. Before I opened the stable door, he cautioned, "Quietly, Mohammed. Do not bother her!"

I asked how he knew I was about to open the stable door so quickly? He sighed deeply and smiled, saying, "You have never entered a place quietly in your life!" He patted my shoulder and led me calmly to sit at the corner of the mare's stable. I wanted to help the mare, so I moved forward to take hold of the little front legs, while he stood aside smiling.

I pulled gently as she pushed, just as Maktoum had taught me. I continued this way until the mare had cleared the head, shoulders and girth of the foal. With one final heave, the baby came tumbling out into my lap. I lifted the newborn as carefully as a piece of china and placed her next to her mother's head while my brother handed me a towel to dry her. I was elated at the miracle in which I had just participated, unable to hold in my feelings of exultation and gratitude to be a witness to a new life coming into the world. I wouldn't have had this amazing experience had it not been for Maktoum.

I sat down, still amazed. Maktoum smiled at me and said, "You are a brilliant assistant, brother. I will call you when all the mares foal from now on."

Content, we sat well into the coming dawn and watched the mare proudly lick her baby. I basked just as proudly in Maktoum's approval of my performance. My brother had just returned for spring break from his studies at language school in Cambridge, where he began studying back in 1960. He told me that at the beginning of his studies, he preferred to remain calm and wait for others to approach him. Maktoum was quiet and conservative, with high morals and self-respect. He seemed to be surrounded by a halo of peace and tranquillity, as if he personified stillness itself.

Conversely, I had an electric current that coursed through me and I could never bear a moment of sitting still. Hamdan, on the other hand was closer to Maktoum's nature, possessing high morals and decency. He was also more academic by character, absorbed by numbers, books and reading.

My memories with Maktoum were many and beautiful. I travelled with him often. We spent countless nights talking and discussing various matters. He possessed wisdom and steadiness, patience and kindness, qualities acknowledged by Sheikh Rashid who commissioned him to deliver the keynote speech at his inauguration ceremony as Ruler of Dubai.

When people heard that Maktoum would be the Crown Prince, they loved him so deeply! They loved him for his grace, softness and proximity to the people.

With my brother Sheikh Maktoum bin Rashid Al Maktoum

Sheikh Maktoum played a key role in the creation of the Union of the United Arab Emirates. His experience and wisdom contributed to solving many of the outstanding problems facing the Union. He also assumed the presidency of its first Council of Ministers. After my father fell ill in the early 1980s, Sheikh Maktoum governed with wisdom, power and clairvoyance. We gave him our support and helped him carry out his responsibilities.

In a meeting with Sheikh Zayed, Sheikh Maktoum and Sheikh Hamdan

One of the many moments I will never forget with my brother Maktoum – may God have mercy on his soul – is the time when he asked me to become the Crown Prince of Dubai. I refused at first, with all due respect. After a while, he repeated his request. We talked for a long time and I explained to him why I had declined this post. I told him that my way of governance would upset many people and could ruin many existing relationships. I also told him explicitly that many people continued to employ the same governance model my father had set up many years ago, unwilling to develop it further because it was what they were used to. Sheikh Maktoum told me that progress was what Dubai really needed. In the end, I convinced him the time was not right for me to assume such a responsibility and we agreed to postpone it.

Four years later, Sheikh Maktoum brought up the same subject again. I will never forget that day! He asked me to become the Crown Prince. He stared at me intently, as if he was trying to tell me that the time had come; as if he was trying to tell me not to let him down this time! I accepted. His eyes filled with tears and he hugged me so tight that to this day I can still feel his arms around me.

Many people ask me, "How did you feel when you woke up the next morning and read the decree of your appointment as a Crown Prince?" The truth is that I did not sleep that night; I did not have time to read the papers. I started working the moment I left the Council.

Sheikh Maktoum knew he could rely on me to work my hardest from the very beginning. Development was a dream to him, but he knew that to me it was an instinct and a matter of life or death.

19

Cambridge

My father did not have a hard time dealing with the British who came to his *majlis*, whether they were military or businessmen. He used to greet them with a smile. It was the same case with the American diplomats and investors, to whom he would tell stories or even jokes. However, all those lengthy sessions in the *majlis* were conducted with the presence of a translator, despite the fact that my father could scatter a few English words here and there throughout his speech.

Although his guests rarely left less than captivated and enchanted, he would often step out of the meetings with frustration showing on his face. He would light his small pipe and take a deep breath, then look seriously at my mother and say, "The kids should go as soon as possible!" As soon as those words were uttered, signs of sadness appeared on her face. That is when he would gently tap her shoulders, saying quietly, "Latifa, I can never make them go through what I experience because of my inability to speak such a language fluently – the language of those we need to help us. They should go as soon as possible."

Learning English was very important to my father. In the 1960s, Dubai started to deal with major foreign companies and developments began at an astonishing speed, including projects my father was launching and major contracts we negotiated. More oil exploration efforts also began to take effect, prior to the discovery of oil off the coast of Dubai in the Fateh oilfield in 1966. It was in this year my father asked me to go to Britain to learn English.

I was avid, in every sense of the word, for all I would see and learn abroad. As soon as they told me that I would be travelling, I did all

I could to get ready. I allocated time each day to study and practise English on my own and made sure to improve with every passing day.

There was not much that I could do, except to always remind myself that I would assume a huge responsibility in my country and that I should not waste a single minute of my time as soon as I arrived in England.

I finally arrived at Mrs Summers' modest house at Brookside in Cambridge in August 1966. I stared at this kindly looking woman and she stared straight back at me. She asked me to follow her to check my room, overwhelming me with a string of words I did not understand. The tone of her voice, however, made me understand that she was offering me friendly words of welcome.

As soon as I closed my door, I was gripped by feelings of longing for my country, my parents and my loved ones. I spent most of my time that first afternoon praying, until Mrs Summers knocked on my door, calling out, "Dinner's ready, Maktoum!" Once the door opened, I was met with strange but interesting smells. Three dishes were put on the table, consisting of meat, mashed potatoes and green peas. We all ate and at the end of the meal, everyone suddenly stood up together, which surprised me. They left me in my place, looking at my plate and wondering what I should do next, until I saw them heading towards the sink to wash up.

I noted with pride that our first meal had been a leg of lamb. I thought that they must be like us Arabs, who prepare a whole animal to serve meat to honoured guests as a sign of hospitality. I stood there trying to be of some use, so I picked up the remainder of the lamb and went to throw it away. I was met with a tirade of unintelligible high-pitched chatter from my hostess.

'They must have other people to feed,' I thought, 'how insensitive of me!' Perhaps she wished to send it to her neighbours. My mother would cook for those in our house and the stream of guests and friends that may pass through. I then noticed that Mrs Summers placed the meat in the fridge. I lived in a society where everyone knew each other. I lived in a society where sharing food with others happened all the time. When we would sit together and enjoy a

Mrs Summers' house in Cambridge, United Kingdom, in 1966

The lively conversations around the kitchen table were one aspect of life in Cambridge that I enjoyed greatly

hearty meal, my mother wrapped any leftovers and took the dish to our neighbours or relatives. This constituted one of the Arabs' most authentic traditions.

The next day, I went with them to explore my new world. I watched the places we were passing and tried to understand the layout of the streets and shops to which Mrs Summers took me. I was going to start my studies at Bell in two days, so we bought all the required books. Then, we returned home for lunch, which was very similar to that of the day before. The lamb was removed from the fridge, heated and served again on the table. They ate it, but with boiled carrots and a side soup this time. I ate, too, with misgivings. In Dubai we always ate food fresh, there were mouths enough to feed at each meal and finish what was there.

I started my studies quickly and added new words to my English vocabulary every day. The more I deepened my mastery of the language and got accustomed to this new place, the greater my knowledge of the Western culture became, and the greater my appreciation for some of its beautiful aspects seemed to be.

Unlike at home where we would stop and stand to salute anyone we encountered, whether a brother, sister or even an employee, in England official salutations were not expected when you met someone you already knew. I was impressed with the simple and modest manner of dealing with people. They never stood up when someone came into the room and seemed a little surprised if someone else did.

The lively conversations around the kitchen table were one aspect of life in Cambridge that I enjoyed greatly. Conversations at mealtimes are more conservative in our culture and I found myself caught up in passionate debates that reflected many opposing opinions but never descended into bad temper.

I also found it strange that people in England never seemed to speak to their neighbours, nor would their neighbours really offer any formal greetings to them. I often tried to greet the people who lived around us, but they looked at me as if I were slightly odd, as I shouted out, "Good morning! Have you any news?" That would have been equivalent to the desert greeting for a perfect stranger, "Assalamu alaikum, peace be upon you. Have you news of faraway lands?"

The time I spent in England still has a special place in my heart. I enjoyed the refreshing mornings and loved the rain, which often fell for days, making the sky seem to weep constantly. I studied hard and did the best I could.

My father managed to kill two
birds with one stone:
to make me learn English, while
also learning the value of money

Mrs Summer's house in Cambridge, United Kingdom, in 1966

I still remember my father's tone when we would talk over the telephone. During each conversation, he never failed to ask me about my progress in mastering English. This made me understand that I was not only in Cambridge to develop my personal skills, but also to fulfil a national service to a country in which many responsibilities awaited me upon my return.

The majority of my time was devoted to studies. I handled the usual and routine duties, as did the rest of the students. I had to pay to turn on the heating in my room and use the telephone. Mrs Summers' family brought me dinner, but I would pay for my lunch from the money my father sent me – two pounds a week.

The money I had was not enough for all weekdays. Usually, I would eat chicken once a week. Sometimes I would skip lunch altogether so I could buy coffee for my friends or – most importantly – pay for a train ticket so I could watch the horse races I loved.

I worked very hard at school and would rake leaves and take on other part-time duties to earn some money so I would be able to go watch the races. My father managed to kill two birds with one stone: to make me learn English, while also learning the value of money.

One day, I received a call that changed my life forever. My father said, "We are holding a very important meeting!" With this sentence, my father meant, "We need you at home – right now!"

I returned to Dubai the next day on the very first available flight.

20

The Northern Tent

My father Sheikh Rashid bin Saeed with Sheikh Zayed bin Sultan

Everything has a beginning, and in the natural order of things, everything comes to an end. Everything, that is, except for great dreams – for although they always have a beginning, they rarely know an end. If you give them your all, they may even outlive you, stretching on for eternity. Our memories of first moments are rare and precious, some details we remember forever with feelings rooted in our souls, and senses of ecstasy and exhilaration that become part of our inner selves. How could we forget the birth of a first child, the first pang of love, the first day at school or a new job? We cherish these memories, they form part of who we are, and who we will become.

In this way, I still remember the birth of the United Arab Emirates as if it were yesterday. The year was 1968. I was pursuing my studies in the ancient city of Cambridge when my father summoned me back home. He asked me to prepare myself to spend a full day in the desert. There, a meeting would be held, away from the prying eyes of spectators and stalkers, far from ill-intentioned people who did not want to see the Union come into being, who did not want to see the scattered tribes of the Trucial States gathered together under the banner of a single nation.

The appointment was with another wise man, one who had been ruling Abu Dhabi for two years – Sheikh Zayed bin Sultan Al Nahyan. Sheikh Zayed was my second father, teacher, mentor and leader for over four decades. From his very first day ruling Abu Dhabi in 1966, he longed for the Union and dreamed of a single state. The discussion aimed to develop a framework for a union between the two emirates, with others subsequently invited to join. It would be a 'fait accompli', a union between Abu Dhabi and Dubai would make it easier for others to follow suit, paving the way for the Union of Arab Emirates.

For years, there had been a lot of talk, futile gatherings and successive alliances in the hope of establishing a single entity. These efforts were always undermined, however, and the dream delayed. This meeting aimed to resolve matters. The two Sheikhs met in Seih Al Sedira between Abu Dhabi and Dubai, marking a historic turning point that transformed the dream of a Union into a reality and constituted a point of no return in the formation of the United Arab Emirates.

I travelled ahead of the two Sheikhs to choose the location. Among my brothers, I possessed the deepest knowledge of the desert and my father therefore trusted my ability to select the most suitable meeting point. I pitched two tents; one for the two Sheikhs to the north, with the doorway oriented so as to welcome a soothing desert breeze – and another to the south for their entourages to stay in. I lit a fire for cooking, while in my heart burned a fire of enthusiasm and excitement for this day, which I knew marked a pivotal moment: one with inevitable repercussions that would shape all our futures. I knew that the words we had been hearing for so long about the establishment of a single state might soon become a living reality. After the preparations were complete, the two Sheikhs arrived along with several companions each. They entered the northern tent alone in order to begin the discussions.

And so it was that the United Arab Emirates first came to life in the northern tent. It was in the northern tent that the two Sheikhs agreed to establish a bilateral Union. It was in the northern tent that the two Sheikhs agreed on the following principles: one common flag, one common healthcare system and one common education system.

First moments are precious –
the birth of a first child,
the first pang of love...
I still remember the birth of
the United Arab Emirates

In the northern tent, something occurred that was almost unprecedented in Arab countries. The two men both declined the presidency, each asking the other to take the role. Sheikh Zayed asked Sheikh Rashid to be the president of the new Union. Sheikh Rashid, smiling and moving his *tasbih* prayer beads, responded, "You are the president!" In the northern tent, long discussions were held on this matter. After much back and forth, Zayed agreed to become the president and Rashid shook his hand in agreement, granting him his full blessing.

Fifty years later, I still remember all that happened in the northern tent with an ache in my heart for the Arab countries that have squandered the precious lives of thousands of their people, wasting billions of dollars and years of progress because of their jostling and fighting for power.

Yes, in the Emirates we are different. Perhaps that is why we have succeeded. Countries succeed when the people's dreams are echoed in

Countries succeed when political
power is used as a means to
cement the people's desires, and
not simply as an end unto itself

My father Sheikh Rashid bin Saeed with Sheikh Zayed bin Sultan

the personal aspirations of their leaders. Countries succeed when leaders abandon their egos to fulfil the hopes of society and achieve great things. Countries succeed when political power is used as a means to cement the people's desires, and not simply as an end unto itself. The United Arab Emirates was founded by altruistic leaders and has seen many miracles come true thanks to their selflessness. One of the enduring secrets of our success is this quality of self-denial for the greater good of the country, which must be embodied by those in charge for this miracle to continue. We must work hard to firmly entrench the values of the Union, the values of Zayed and Rashid. In the United Arab Emirates, no single person is greater than the Union, no dream is greater than consolidating the Union and no ambitions are worthier than those that bring benefit to the Union.

As the historic meeting between Zayed and Rashid came to an end, the Union between Abu Dhabi and Dubai was declared, prompting international reactions over the next few days. King Hussein of Jordan was among those who offered their compliments. Kuwait and Saudi Arabia also offered their best wishes as did the British, extending warm and yet guarded congratulations.

My father rejoiced at the achievement of bringing the Union of Arab Emirates to the point of conception. However, signs of exhaustion and fatigue began to appear on his face. After a long silence, while we made our way back from Seih Al Sedira following that momentous occasion, he said, "Mohammed, the new-born Union will require protection from enemies, both within and without. We have agreed with Sheikh Zayed to establish a federal entity responsible for defence and internal security. I want you to be responsible for protecting our Union."

21
An Historic Responsibility

With my father Sheikh Rashid bin Saeed Al Maktoum

The life of every human is defined by moments that separate one phase from another, one life from another, the end of one dream from the beginning of another. In my life, the key instant that separated my youth from my manhood was a single, simple sentence delivered by Sheikh Rashid: "Mohammed, we want you to be responsible for protecting the Union."

I had heard and read about great leaders throughout our history who had led armies when they were still young, such as Usama bin Zayd and Qutayba bin Muslim. Yet I regarded these inspiring stories as mere historical fantasy, heroic legends from our beautiful past.

That was until a similar responsibility was conferred upon me at only 19 years old: to establish an army for a state that did not have its own military, to prepare a defence plan for a state that had not yet been born, to strive to unify the forces of seven separate emirates that had not yet built trust among each other. In 1971, we would need an army to fill the void soon to be left by the imminent withdrawal of British forces; an army that could provide protection for this newly born nation in a troubled region, where ambitions for expansion, political intrigue and war were rampant forces.

Defence constituted one of the most delicate issues raised during the talks about founding the Union, concerning both domestic and foreign defence. I was fully aware of the sensitivity of the matter, as well as of the importance of the duty I was about to assume.

To my surprise, I was not afraid of the responsibility, but I was keenly aware that it would mean elevating my abilities, my thinking and my potential to levels I had never before imagined.

Work started immediately. Sheikh Rashid issued a decree appointing me as the Head of Dubai Police and Public Security in February 1968. My father also wanted to send me for specialist military training. Of course, there was no country better regarded than the United Kingdom, with whose military practices we were all familiar. I believed that they had the most extensive military expertise in the world. I had often considered how this country gained control over one quarter of the globe, earning its title of 'the empire on which the sun never sets'. I wondered about the kind of training that British army officers received. I wanted the very best military training I could get.

I spoke to my father about formalising the last step of my military training at that point, and it was agreed that I would leave as soon as possible for England. I travelled to the military training establishment at Beaconsfield in Buckinghamshire for my evaluation. The results of the physical and aptitude assessments shocked me and led to an unexpected outcome. The Commanding Officer invited me into his office and asked me to be seated. He explained that the skills taught at Beaconsfield were ones I had already achieved. There was no reason for me to enrol, there was nothing they could teach me. "Even though," he continued, "a large part of our training here is physical, you have been assessed as being in better shape than the majority of your supervisors. I suggest you review your decision to enrol."

I understood by the genuine way in which the Commanding Officer had spoken to me that this was not a rebuff or a dismissal, but I had no idea where to go or what to do at that point. I was delighted, of course, but also rather mystified. I took a taxi back to London and during the journey decided to ask for a meeting at the Ministry of

I was determined not to return to Dubai until I was physically, mentally and militarily capable of facing anything

During the graduation of a military course in 1977

Defence. After listening to me and checking with Beaconsfield, they suggested I enrol at the Mons Officer Cadet School in Aldershot. I was overjoyed with this choice and called my father to tell him the good news. The best thing about it was that training at Mons was much tougher than Beaconsfield. I knew I'd have to give it maximum effort, for I was determined not to return to Dubai until I was physically, mentally and militarily capable of facing anything. I was ready for them to put me through the hardest training they could throw at me!

The 161 Infantry Officer Cadet Training Unit was part of the Royal Military Academy, Sandhurst, and was later renamed the Mons Officer Cadet School. The 161 Unit cadets were known as a tough crowd. Mons remained the main training base for the British cavalry regiments and artillery and, a few years after I left, was amalgamated into Sandhurst. I joined the Kohima Company, along with other officers of the Household Cavalry, Royal Engineers, guards and infantry. They found it difficult to pronounce my name – Mohammed bin Rashid Al Maktoum. The Officer in Command, eventually followed by all the others, decided to call me 'Officer Rashid'. Except for when he got especially furious (which was often), then he would simply scream, 'Maktoum!'

When I first arrived, they had no idea who I was, which initially worked in my favour. My life became much harder the moment my direct Officer in Charge learned my identity. It's a hard thing to describe, but that's what happened. I believe he was afraid that the others would think he treated me differently, out of favouritism or something similar. Despite everything, I loved hardship and fatigue and learned

With my father Sheikh Rashid bin Saeed Al Maktoum

how to endure physical pain. This is what I had come for, even if the price to pay was cracked skin from the cold, sleep deprivation and precious little time for eating. As for medical examinations, handling weapons, shooting and map reading, the desert had given me a powerful foundation that helped me meet and eventually master all these skills.

Throughout it all, I could hear my father's voice in my mind, heart and soul at every moment, telling me, "You will be responsible for protecting the Union!" His words gave me unparalleled energy, even as I required my undivided focus to master all the lessons. I did so without hesitation – it was a small price to pay for my nation.

22

Kohima

I have a particular personality trait: I'm highly competitive by nature. I'm not exactly sure where it came from, whether it was innate or acquired. Competing with others drives me to be stronger and more determined.

My goal is always to be in first place, and I always strive for this – even when I'm not aware I'm doing so. Perhaps this was inspired by my lifelong love of horse racing. Or perhaps it's the other way around and it is this innate trait that has enabled me to win with horses – and other races in my life.

It was surely our desire, perhaps even our destiny, to be part of establishing a state, which we would always strive to push into first place. Even before its inception, this nation would instil within us the love of first place.

At Mons Officer Cadet School in Aldershot, United Kingdom, in 1968

I started training with the Kohima Company at the Mons Officer Cadet School, and I had a singular goal: to graduate first in my class. I wanted to make my country proud.

Kohima Company was sent on its first exercise to Dartmoor. There was apprehension at the barracks, I remember, because it was known to be so tough. I did not feel apprehensive, however, because I was used to the harsh environment of the desert. I knew how to tackle its rugged and wild nature. In the desert there are very few landmarks, unlike the variable landscape of England's countryside, which is rather easier to navigate for the *Bedouin* eye.

My training at Mons covered a range of military doctrines, as well as the use of weapons, knowledge of different communication tools, and modern warfare methods and strategies. I strived to always give my best and to excel in all areas of physical, mental and military training. I was close to getting full marks when something unexpected happened.

On the eve of our last exercise, which was to take place on the Brecon Beacons, we had to undergo a full inspection. I was in charge of leading my company and stood in front. The Sergeant Major had decided I was two steps left of my company, but I did not believe I could have made such a basic mistake at this advanced stage of training. By now, the Brigadier General had arrived. As we waited, I dropped my eyes and concentrated on a chalk mark drawn on the parade ground in front of where I stood. "Officerrrrrrrrr CADET Raaaaaaaaashid! Two Stepsssss to the Left!" the Sergeant Major boomed.

I'm not sure why I reacted. Perhaps it was based on the injustice of being caught out and publicly humiliated in front of my men. In any event, I reacted.

"KohyeeeeMa! Two Steps to the Riiiight!" I shouted in a loud clear voice that echoed, I hoped, as far as the sand dunes of Dubai. The entire company behind me moved two steps to the right and fell in line. The Sergeant Major looked furious and behind me I knew the

At Mons Officer Cadet School in Aldershot, United Kingdom, in 1968

other officer cadets would mentally be laying bets on the punishment I would receive. The Brigadier was very complimentary at the lunch that followed, praising my initiative and the obvious leadership skills that Mons imparted to its intake. The Sergeant Major seemed to like that part and no disciplinary action was taken after all.

Two weeks prior to graduation we were sent on exercises in Wales. The examinations were harder and the training more intense than ever. During those 12 days, I exerted every possible effort in the hope of making up for any previous shortcomings. I applied all of my skills and experience in the Welsh hills, in the hope that my grades would not suffer.

On October 18th, 1968, my father attended my graduation parade. When he went to meet Colonel Brooks, who was in charge of the

Kohima Company, Mons Officer Cadet School in 1968

> **My father looked at me and his eyes shone with a pride that seemed to well up from the depths of his soul. When he looked at me, I felt as though time stood still**

Mons Officer Cadet School, the Colonel told him that my grades were high in all disciplines.

My father looked at me and his eyes shone with a pride that seemed to well up from the depths of his soul. When he looked at me, I felt as though time stood still, and that I had given him the greatest gift of all during those difficult years before the Union was established.

I whispered in his ear that I would be by his side during the ceremony to translate for him. He told me, "No, Mohammed. I will be the one by your side today. You will be by my side in Dubai, for we have three years to equip an army prior to the British withdrawal and I now have a military commander standing in front of me whom I trust with this responsibility."

23

Help from God

During the performance of *Umrah*

"Mohammed, you will be responsible for protecting the Union."
It was a sensitive responsibility, especially after the British announced their intention to withdraw within only three years. They may have been betting on our inability to protect ourselves. However, my father and Sheikh Zayed held a very different view.

In November 1968, my father asked me to establish a federal defence force that could protect our nascent state. After my father told me his decision, there was a moment of complete silence after which I kissed his forehead and promised him I would protect our homeland with all my heart and soul. I then asked for my father's permission to go to Mecca to perform *Umrah* and spend a few days in the Holy City. I needed clarity and guidance, the harmonisation between my intentions and the will of God. I was, and still am, in need of the help of God and His guidance in all of my affairs.

Throughout my 50 years of service, I have witnessed many miracles in my homeland resulting from being in harmony with God's will. I have witnessed the protection and care for my homeland by the Sustainer of all beings. I have witnessed wars and upheaval and the collapse of countries that were thousands of years old. While my homeland – with the hand of God and His guardianship – flourished, embodying a marvel of development and progress. Vanity, delusions of grandeur and believing in one's own strength and limited power are some of humankind's worst traits. We must acknowledge Divine power over everything. We strive, but success comes from God. We act, but direction and support are delivered by Him. We purify our motives to serve people, but it is the Sustainer of all beings who grants us accomplishments in accordance with our intentions. Guidance, care and protection all come from God.

> **❝**
> Vanity, delusions of
> grandeur and believing in one's
> own strength and limited power
> are some of humankind's
> worst traits
> **❞**

In Mecca, I sat alone in contemplation. I prayed and sought God's grace. In Mecca, the whirlwind of my thoughts was calmed. I was overcome by clarity and tranquillity and started to contemplate the answers to many of the significant questions before me.

What would it take to establish a strong defence force quickly? What were the main threats to the emerging state? How could I identify the forces that sought to destabilise or ultimately overthrow the nation? How could a military force be built without affecting the limited financial resources that a fledgling nation would need for development? Where should I begin, and how? Who could I rely on? Where would I be in three years? I needed to take every possible scenario into account.

There, under the stars of Mecca the blessed, many resolutions were revealed to me and the main features of my plan began to emerge. I started to see the future, day by day, year by year, and a clear vision for the next three years of my life began to form.

God on high, I kneel to Your name.
    You are the one true God, a glimpse from You would fulfil me.
My mortal body kneels before Your glory.
    I have taken off the trappings of kings with trembling hands.
My yearning has been here for so long.
    The voice of truth whispers to my solitude.
And I have followed that voice.
I came seeking forgiveness in Mecca in all humility.
    Owner of the universe You met me with mercy.
Brightness filled me.
    Lord, creator of light, You are my guide.
I stood and the night witnessed my long deprivation.
    God, look on me and don't leave me lonely.

24

Seas, Deserts, Skies & Men

There is a famous saying of the scientist, philosopher and artist Leonardo da Vinci, "Simplicity is the ultimate sophistication."

I am a great believer in this principle. However, you cannot simplify an elaborate plan unless you first have acquired a thorough understanding of it. You cannot explain a complicated theory to a child unless you have truly grasped all of its details. You cannot attain wisdom in life unless you fully comprehend complex facts, situations and lessons, and can summarise them in straightforward words that thousands of people will understand and use. This is true wisdom.

Simplicity is hard. It is easy to write a lengthy letter explaining a problem. But it is difficult to pare it down to just one verse. This is why poetry is so very complex. Each word is packed with meaning. It is easy to fill thousands of papers with great plans for the future. However, it is difficult to put them in simple words that people can understand, believe in and uphold, and even make personal sacrifices for these words.

During the graduation ceremony for soldiers in Manama Camp

After much thought, I set out a strategy to build an internal police force in preparation for establishing a comprehensive defence force covering the main areas of: sea, desert, sky and manpower. We had maritime borders that urgently needed to be protected using speedboats, a range of communication equipment and radars. We had open desert and land borders that needed protection by ensuring rapid access to a variety of troop carriers and tanks, as well as communication equipment and other assets. Then we had the skies – the most difficult and important element – it's no secret that control of the skies is critical to modern defence.

From the beginning, I decided the emphasis would be placed on training for ground combat, then build our air force and navy once the financial conditions became favourable. For each of these areas,

Enrolment of recruits in educational classes in Dubai in 1971

> ## You cannot attain wisdom in life unless you fully comprehend complex facts, situations and lessons

thousands of details had to be taken into consideration and dealt with, for which I drew on the lessons I had learned during my military training. It also involved bringing international best practices and expertise to bear.

'Men' constituted the most difficult element of the plan, for they are always the most important and most critical component of any endeavour, be it the army, the government or even the private sector. If you are not careful in choosing your human resources, if you do not truly build their capabilities and skills, or if you fail to provide them with the strongest values or motivate them and instil a spirit of enthusiasm in them, then you will fail from day one.

By the end of the 1960s, we had only a few dozen police officers in Dubai and the same number in the defence force as well. I wanted to start with at least 1,000 men, but I did not just want any thousand. I wanted 1,000 men to serve as the core of the other tens of thousands who would come after them. I wanted 1,000 men who would be capable of building all branches of our armed forces later on.

I wanted 1,000 of the elite. I placed great importance on the reputation of this elite, both inside and outside the United Arab Emirates. In short, I wanted 1,000 men who were worth 10,000.

We established the Dubai Defence Force in 1971. I announced the vacancies available in the Dubai Defence Force, stating that acceptance would be based solely on skill. We also launched a widespread door-to-door campaign to encourage people to enlist. In the spirit of our culture, we wrote poems to pay tribute to this new force, using various means to motivate the people and instil in them a sense of patriotism. So the work began. Young people came forward, first in tens and then in their hundreds. We selected the most suitable and apt candidates. I promised all recruits a good education along with the training. Many recruits were illiterate young men who showed a great interest and desire to learn, for they strongly believed in the importance of education. To that end, I recruited teachers from Dubai schools to cover this aspect of my plan.

My strategy focused on three pillars: physical training, military combat skills and education. Thus, we embarked on our journey to build a strong and capable defence force. I developed a rigorous training programme, similar to my experience at the Mons Officer Cadet School. Accordingly, recruits' days were divided into balanced periods, intended to cover all topics. I did, however, adapt and develop the programme to reflect our local conditions in Dubai.

The men's spirits were high, and I accompanied them every step of the way, through all the different stages of training. The men would never listen to a leader who was not prepared to get his hands dirty.

I used to run with them, break sweat with them, eat with them. I was with them during all the tough exercises and I personally ensured they received the right uniforms, the right education and the right combat plans. I shared with them my knowledge of the desert, and I learned from them too. I gave them all my energy, and – in return – they gave me the best force in existence at that time.

I remember during the early stages of my work, the British representative telling me, 'Mohammed, you are inexperienced and need supervision.' The next day, as he arrived at his office, I had a guard placed on the door. After two quiet days, he got the message and I asked him to leave.

My troops showed me loyalty and love, because they saw that I worked around the clock. The training would start in the yard at exactly 8am. In the afternoon, I used to work with them at exactly the same time that I used to work with my father before attending council meetings.

As for the nights, they were much longer. If the telephone rang, I would answer at the ready. No sooner had I changed my clothes to sleep for a few hours than I was up again, putting on fresh clothes and rushing out to the next task that awaited me. During that period of my life, my only periods of tranquillity were during prayer and thinking about my beloved horses.

The hard work paid off, however, and in just two years, the number of police and defence force officers increased dramatically. We now had a trained force of 1,000 men who were indeed worth 10,000.

25

The Arabic Pipe

Sheikh Rashid bin Saeed Al Maktoum

In January 1968, the British Prime Minister Harold Wilson announced the United Kingdom's intention to withdraw from the Gulf because of an accelerating decline in the British economy. In particular the devaluation of sterling by 14 per cent in November 1967 had, at a stroke, increased the costs of maintaining British forces 'east of Suez'. This made Britain's continued presence in the Gulf similarly costly. Wilson's announcement meant withdrawal from the Gulf within three years. The political signals we were receiving, however, expressed the United Kingdom's clear desire to maintain some foothold in the region which, of course, was home to the world's largest oil resources. In this respect, the Americans and the British saw the region as a political issue and potentially an area of conflict between the West and the Soviet Union.

We noticed these ominous signs of continued presence through the messages the British Government was sending: that we were unable to protect ourselves, that our people were growing impatient with the pace of establishing the Union; all potentially damaging and all highly misleading. Clearly, the British had desires and ambitions for the region, even after withdrawal. My father was disturbed by these signals and requested a meeting with Wilson in the summer of 1969. As our meeting started, I found it amusing to hear the conversation go back and forth between Wilson's broad Yorkshire accent and my father's *Bedouin* accent. I sat and listened to them talk about many important matters, my father clearly expressing our need to have total autonomy over our decisions.

Wilson took out his trademark pipe and filled it with tobacco while he was thinking. I saw the relief in my father's face as he also lit his own pipe. He must have previously assumed that it was inappropriate to smoke as long as his host did not smoke or invite him to do so. The Arabic pipe is a far smaller version of the English model. However, the quality of tobacco used by the Arabs is so strong that a single puff is plenty. The two men relaxed as they smoked and talked about the region. My father finished his first puff of the pipe and gently rested it on the ashtray. Wilson looked at his pipe, then smiled. He nodded towards his pipe and said, "Look, my pipe is much bigger than yours."

My father smiled, then looked at me and said, "Tell Wilson that I agree with him – his pipe is bigger than mine. But even though my pipe is small, the tobacco I use is very strong and powerful."

Clearly, the two men were not talking about their pipes. This was the subtle language of politicians, conveying unspoken messages. Wilson's words reflected the United Kingdom's great size compared to our nation, as well as its almost unchallenged ability to act as it wished. My father's message was very clear: do not underestimate us because of our size, for we are strong and have a determination that may not be visible to you – we are more than capable of protecting ourselves.

The talks ended on a positive note. We returned to Dubai, believing that we had been able to build bridges of understanding with the British, and had ensured that the withdrawal would happen within the promised timeframe. That is until an unexpected event took place a year or so later. In the spring of 1970, general elections were held in the United Kingdom. Our friend from Yorkshire was unexpectedly defeated by Edward Heath's Conservative Government, who won with an overall majority of 31 seats in the House of Commons.

With the British Prime Minister Harold Wilson in 1969

At first, this victory was a source of concern for us, since statements made by Heath during the election campaign indicated that the Conservatives wished British forces to remain in the Gulf to fulfil its global commitments and to protect oil reserves. Tensions flared: having started on the road to independence, we could not accept a continued British political presence and we made sure that this message was conveyed to Heath. It was not until March 1971 that I was able to breathe a sigh of relief, with reassurances we received from political sources in London. Accordingly, Heath officially announced that he would not change national policy and that the United Kingdom would, indeed, withdraw from the area.

Politicians speak the language of diplomatic expediency, whereas facts speak the language of strength. We were determined to build this strength at all costs, after all was said and done; that was my father's mission in life. The great responsibility that lay before me was to build this strength through which our new-born nation could communicate with the rest of the world.

26

A Race
Against Time
(& Consultants)

Meeting with Sheikh Zayed bin Sultan and my father Sheikh Rashid bin Saeed

From 1969 to 1971, we were in a race against time to finalise an Arab agreement of great significance; an agreement that is still in force to this day and whose ultimate outcome was the foundation of the United Arab Emirates; the only viable Arab country conceived by genuine union, rather than arbitrary lines drawn on a map. The UAE is the only country that was built by Arab leaders through agreement rather than force; the only country that has shown how successful the outcome can be when Arabs agree and work together to build a common future for their people. The only country that defies the spirit of tribalism and faction, disguised as sectarian, religious or ethnic divisions. Such a spirit still exists in so many of our Arab neighbours. This ancestral character is still deeply entrenched inside us, as reflected in the verse:

I am but from a tribe, if it errs, so do I,
and if it is rightly guided then so am I.

Even today we maintain a close-knit and protectionist tribal nature. And, as another poet said:

We only drink if water is pure,
while others drink from murky depths.

The Union of the United Arab Emirates is thus an exception to contemporary Arab history, based on friendly and mutually beneficial agreements between its peoples, without bloodshed. This feat has, sadly, never been celebrated or replicated in the rest of the Arab world. Our feelings, three years before our Union, fluctuated between an intense enthusiasm for the new dream and disappointment in some of those neighbouring countries we thought were our friends.

There were also occasional fears that we would not conclude the agreement on time, missing an historic opportunity that might never be repeated. In this situation, Sheikh Zayed and Sheikh Rashid were the two main pillars upon whom we all relied. Together, they formed the foundations of our faith and belief in the Union when disappointment and challenges arose. Those years witnessed some intense political activity, during which I was a constant companion to my father. He entrusted me with numerous tasks and asked me to represent him, along with my brother Sheikh Maktoum, in many negotiations. We would speak on his behalf and with his authority. This conferred upon us strength and respect, and it was a valuable lesson in the importance of delegating authority to those you trust to carry out tasks and fulfil responsibilities.

My father was determined to form a federation consisting of the seven emirates as well as Qatar and Bahrain. He was always pushing to complete this before 1971. To that end, the rulers met in Jumeirah on February 25th, 1968, where they formed a Federal Supreme Council and began to conduct detailed negotiations. Another meeting of the Federal Supreme Council was held in July of the same year, resulting in the institution of the Interim Federal Council.

My brother, Crown Prince Sheikh Maktoum, was to represent Dubai in the council. There were many pending issues, such as the distribution of power, budgets and other matters. Despite the intense pressures we were subjected to, we carried out numerous lengthy and difficult negotiations. We persevered, despite the rumours that our peoples were dissatisfied with their rulers and constant media reports attacking our governments, accusing us of failing to exert real efforts for the sake of the Union. We carried on calmly despite the hearsay, gossip and even threats of military intervention.

Luckily, many saw that a state with great potential, supported by abundant oil reserves, was on the verge of being born, while others saw only a nation to be seized and controlled to ensure their own interests. As for us, we saw only the need to carry on resolutely, step by step. My father met with all the Gulf Sheikhs, while maintaining his own responsibilities. I attended these meetings. They all wished the burgeoning United Arab Emirates great success, which encouraged us to pursue what we had started and to reassure our people that we were on the right path to a strong, new state, God willing.

During a meeting with advisors in the presence of my father Sheikh Rashid

I told my father frankly that the consultants would end up destroying the idea of the Union

My father, my brothers and I worked together like a relay team, never hesitating for a moment to exert all necessary efforts and all too aware of the urgent need to achieve tremendous results in that short timeframe. In May 1969, we attended a third meeting of the Federal Supreme Council held in Qatar, with the aim of forming the Union. The main issues of disagreement revolved around the parliamentary entity and its structure, the Federal National Council, as well as the equal representation of all emirates. Appropriate solutions to all these issues had to be reached. In the end, we all had to compromise a little to successfully forge the Union. In Dubai, we agreed on proportional representation, marking one of the defining moments in the formation of our new nation.

Consultants representing the various emirates started to develop and document the agreements that were concluded between the rulers according to their final, detailed framework. They also embarked upon endless amendments and discussions that made it feel like the dream of the Union would not be achieved anytime soon. The legal hurdles that they set to the formation of the Union also increased day after day. I watched all of this happen with the utmost disgust. I knew

During a meeting with my brothers, Sheikh Hamdan and Sheikh Maktoum, in 1971

they did not want the negotiations to end or the Union to be born, for that would mark the end of their involvement and more important, an end to the profits they gained from these constant tours, visits and negotiations. But, sometimes, all you have is patience and wisdom to overcome the obstacles people place in your way. I told my father frankly that the consultants would end up destroying the idea of the Union. They traded in information and rumours, and were trying their best to deepen divisions, rather than resolve them. I simply despised this. However, I was confident and certain that we had reached a point where the Union was no longer a choice nor an option but, rather, a destiny and a certainty.

We were in a real race against time and the British withdrawal deadline. We held many talks with Whitehall to confirm the United Kingdom's withdrawal and affirm our ability to protect ourselves. We were also in a race with the rest of the emirates to agree on all outstanding issues and matters related to the founding of the state. Finally, we were in a race against the consultants to finalise the legal frameworks of those agreements. Those years were crucial to building our state, making our dream come true and creating a future for the people of the United Arab Emirates.

27

The Declaration of the Union

The Founding Fathers of the United Arab Emirates

There are moments recorded in history which hold so many accomplishments they cannot be properly conveyed in words. One such moment was the declaration of the Union of the United Arab Emirates. Through constant hard work and steely determination, we were able to seize a truly historic moment of unity in the long journey of Arab collaboration, which has been marked out by so many dreams, failures and raw emotions.

We resumed the series of lengthy meetings on the formation of the proposed Union and decided to hold a summit in Abu Dhabi in October 1969 in the presence of the nine members. The summit's agenda included several points, namely the election of the President and Vice President, the selection of the federal capital and the formation of the Federal National Council. All these matters required prolonged dialogue and a practical perspective to bear fruit.

At the start of the meeting, Sheikh Zayed said, "We have gathered today, in Abu Dhabi, with an historic opportunity before us. We can face the uncertainty of the future together. Let us not forget the consequences we could suffer if we fail to seize the opportunity before us."

These words paved the way for fruitful meetings. Sheikh Zayed was elected President and Sheikh Rashid became Vice President. Qatar's Crown Prince, Sheikh Khalifa bin Hamad Al Thani, was elected Prime Minister and Abu Dhabi was declared the interim capital of the country. The British would soon spoil our exuberance by sending a statement from the Political Resident in Bahrain, Sir Stewart Crawford. Anger overtook some of the participants in the meeting who then left the room. All our efforts were in vain.

In a meeting of UAE Rulers

As I watched the meeting fall apart before my eyes, I remember that I looked at my hands resting in my lap. This breakdown meant that, with just 24 months to go before the United Kingdom's withdrawal, I had to consider the possibility that Dubai would be left standing on its own. I was not happy about this at all. But duty dictated that I had to maintain its security no matter what. I simply had to make even greater efforts to build Dubai's police and defence forces.

The dream began to fade even further when Qatar published a provisional constitution on April 2nd, 1970, and formed a cabinet. Bahrain also decided to move forward on its own. On August 14th, 1971, Bahrain declared its independence and applied for recognition as a state by the United Nations and the League of Arab States. On September 3rd of that same year, Qatar followed suit.

We Emiratis were the first to congratulate them and wish them success. If the Union had not been blessed with success, there is no doubt that we all would have gone the same route, for it was the only option under which our sovereignty would not be compromised.

During April and May 1971, my brothers and I worked tirelessly to persuade everyone to reach an agreement. Of course we faced setbacks, as was the case on July 10th, 1971, during a meeting of the Trucial States Council in Dubai, which I attended along with Sheikh Maktoum. The talks lasted seven days until on Sunday, July 18th, 1971, we issued the following statement:

> "In response to the will of our Arab people, we, the rulers of the emirates of Abu Dhabi, Dubai, Sharjah, Ajman, Umm Al Quwain and Fujairah, have decided to form an independent, sovereign federal state; the United Arab Emirates. On this blessed day, the United Arab Emirates Interim Constitution was signed, and as we make this joyous announcement to the Arab people, we ask God that this Union constitutes the core of a more comprehensive one, that includes the rest of the sister emirates, whom circumstances have prevented from signing this Constitution."

Circumstances were indeed far from in our favour, and when we would sit and talk after a day's work, holding debriefing sessions with my father late into the night, everything was as clear as day. We urgently needed to achieve several priorities before the British withdrawal – namely building a stable economy and a strong defence force able to handle the troubled region, as well as ensuring safety and security, and

> There are moments recorded in history which hold so many accomplishments they cannot be properly conveyed in words. One such moment was the declaration of the Union of the United Arab Emirates.

With the Founding Father Sheikh Zayed bin Sultan

developing a single voice with which to speak, so as to establish a whole, unified nation. Despite it all, we were able to mobilise the people and meet under the same roof, and thus we succeeded in achieving our goal. On December 1st, 1971, the British Political Resident conducted his last tour of the Trucial States, and then terminated all the treaties concluded with Britain since the General Maritime Treaty of 1820, including its pledge to protect the United Arab Emirates.

On December 2nd, 1971, the rulers of Abu Dhabi, Dubai, Sharjah, Ajman, Umm Al Quwain and Fujairah met at Sheikh Rashid's palace in Dubai. In a closed session, the rulers unanimously elected Sheikh Zayed as President, Sheikh Rashid as Vice President and my brother, Sheikh Maktoum, the Crown Prince of Dubai, as the Prime Minister. The following historical statement was issued:

> "On this Thursday, December 2nd, 1971, here in the emirate of Dubai, the rulers of Abu Dhabi, Dubai, Sharjah, Ajman, Umm Al Quwain and Fujairah met as signatories to the United Arab Emirates Interim Constitution, in an atmosphere of sincere brotherhood, mutual trust and firm determination to achieve the aspirations of the people of the United Arab Emirates, and have issued a declaration, under which the terms and conditions of the aforementioned Constitution enter into force, effective on this date."

The rulers then continued their meeting under the Federal Supreme Council. His Highness Sheikh Zayed bin Sultan Al Nahyan, Ruler of Abu Dhabi, was elected President of the United Arab Emirates for a five-year term, and His Highness Sheikh Rashid bin Saeed Al Maktoum,

Ruler of Dubai, was elected Vice President for the same period of time. Sheikh Zayed bin Sultan Al Nahyan and Sheikh Rashid bin Saeed Al Maktoum took the oath under the provisions of the Constitution. Sheikh Maktoum bin Rashid Al Maktoum, Crown Prince of Dubai, was appointed Prime Minister. The Council would hold its second meeting in Abu Dhabi on Tuesday, December 7th, 1971.

"The Federal Supreme Council bears good news for the people of the United Arab Emirates, the Arab sister countries and all other nations around the world. Today, we are witnessing the establishment of the United Arab Emirates as an independent, sovereign state and part of a greater Arab nation. The United Arab Emirates aims to maintain its independence, sovereignty, security and stability in defence against any potential attack on any member of the Emirati people. The United Arab Emirates also seeks to protect the freedoms and rights of its people, and to enhance cooperation between the different emirates, so as to preserve the public interests of all. In addition to the aforementioned goals, the United Arab Emirates aims to work to achieve the prosperity and progress of the nation in all fields, ensuring a better life for all its citizens, as well as providing the support required to defend Arab causes and interests, as well as the Charter of the United Nations in line with international conventions.

In this respect, the Union condemns the use of force, and expresses its regret over Iran's recent occupation of part of the Arab nation[1]. Accordingly, the Union considers it the utmost necessity to uphold legal rights, and resolve conflicts and disputes arising between nations, through the adoption of globally recognised and accepted means.

On this blessed, historic occasion, the Federal Supreme Council would like to extend its gratitude and great praise to God, the Almighty, for His help and support in achieving this joyous outcome. The Federal Supreme Council would also like to extend its warmest congratulations and blessings to the people of the Union on the achievement of security and safety, which came as a result of their belief in the Council, affirming that any form of unity in this part of the world shall constitute a step on the right path towards achieving full Arab unity. The Union reaffirms its commitment to welcoming any other Arab country wishing to join the United Arab Emirates, especially the sister emirates, which signed the UAE Union Agreement in Dubai on February 28th, 1968."

We still welcome any Arab country that wishes to join, as we believe the Union's path is towards prosperity and strength for the people. Even if we are not united by land, why not be united by heart?

On December 16th, 1971, I went with Sheikh Maktoum, the Prime Minister, to Abu Dhabi to attend the first meeting of the Federal Council of the new government, in which I was appointed as Minister of Defence. The youngest minister in the world at the time, at 22, I had the job of building a military force to protect the newly born Union.

---

1 On November 30th, 1971, the Imperial Iranian Navy sent forces to take over three islands; Abu Musa and the Greater and Lesser Tunbs, following British withdrawal.

28

What Will Come After Independence?

With my father Sheikh Rashid bin Saeed Al Maktoum

Looking back on the questions we asked ourselves about what comes next in the Gulf in the early 1970s, it is now clear that the answers serve as powerful portents to many of the events that have rocked the Arab world since then. Most of the Arab countries were free of their British or French colonial masters by the second half of the 20th century, often following prolonged struggles for independence. New freedoms to control their resources and destinies did not always bring direct benefits, as infant nations frequently lacked the stable institutions they needed to manage their economies and public services. Not least of the challenges left in the wake of colonialisation was that of arbitrary national borders left behind by the departing powers, creating time bombs for future conflicts.

Good management has allowed some nations to ascend to the peaks, whereas bad management has caused others to fall to the bottom of the sea. We often blame the colonialists for our developmental regression, our absurd wars, our decrepit economies, and even for our cultural and educational deterioration. However, we have only ourselves to blame. We are the ones who resisted taking up the reins of good government after they left.

I was there when the last of the British soldiers left the Royal Air Force Base in Sharjah. The British left after 150 years of heavy presence in our region, during which time they paid little attention to the developmental needs of our people. I was charged with receiving everything they left behind, including their defence responsibilities. Upon the departure of the last aircraft, our soldiers shouted with much pride and joy. On that day I got a taste of complete freedom, the freedom to manage the internal and external affairs of our country, our economic and developmental matters.

The feeling of complete freedom was paired with another feeling; I felt a heaviness, the sense of absolute responsibility.

I used to travel extensively between all the emirates as part of my primary task of building a unified defence force. Many of our people were living in harsh conditions, especially in those emirates that had scarce resources. They were forced to drink unclean water from wells, which led to a high rate of child mortality. We did not have enough schools or hospitals. We did not have a proper network of roads to link all the emirates. We used to consider clean drinking water and electricity as luxuries.

Once the establishment of the Union was announced, there was a new sense of hope among the people. There was a spirit abroad, eager for change and with a view of the future in their hopeful eyes. We were a nation that looked forward to a rest following our hardship, to health after illness, and to education after ignorance. We were a nation that saw in the Union a respite after all the years of suffering we had endured.

During my daily tours of the various military facilities across the emirates, I was determined to meet as many Emirati families as I could. We had a good stock of supplies, and I used to distribute these to the families. I would enter their homes and see for myself that the road to changing the life of these people for the better would be a long one. My visits to these people made me determined to limit the budget for defence and the military as much as I could, because we needed funds to build schools, clinics, roads, and housing, and had an even more urgent need to invest in developing our nation's people. Sheikh Zayed and Sheikh Rashid used to amend the defence budget, sometimes increasing it, because they were aware that I was being cautious in order to divert the funds to the Union's budget for developmental projects, which they were supervising themselves. Sheikh Zayed and Sheikh Rashid both saw what I was seeing. They had a better sense than I did of what the people actually needed. That is why they left the task of building the defence force to me, and fought the developmental battles themselves, because they were the most pressing.

No country can consider its military strength more important than the welfare and comfort of its people. This may sound strange coming from the Minister of Defence, but if a balance is not achieved, then the army will be charged with protecting a group of miserable people and a barren landscape. The essence of any country's power lies less in its military strength than in its reach, knowledge and development. I see countries like North Korea that have some of the mightiest military forces in the world yet whose peoples are poor, sometimes to the point of starvation. At the same time, countries like South Korea or Japan do not have big armies, but the power of their economies means they stand shoulder to shoulder with the greatest of nations.

God Almighty graced us with the wisdom of the Union's founding leaders, enabling us to balance our spending for military purposes and developmental progress, to balance our internal battle to build and our external battle to improve relations and avoid conflicts, and to balance building structures with the building up of our people. The day after the colonialists depart is the day you choose your battles. Some countries chose the wrong battles, but we were blessed with Sheikh Zayed and Sheikh Rashid, who chose theirs well.

29

A Single Army for a Unified Nation

One of the most challenging tasks I have undertaken during my career was building a unified defence force for the new state.

The army is the force that deters foreign threats, maintains internal cohesion and protects against chaos in times of crisis. It is the protector of everything we have achieved so far and the assurance of stability, which is so vital to investor confidence. The army is what guarantees we are respected among other nations and are protected.

In the case of the United Arab Emirates, the main challenge was to build a defence force that would discourage foreign enemies, ensure stability within and work towards unifying the forces of all seven emirates under one federal umbrella. This was at the top of the list for the initial five-year term of the federal government in 1971.

My plan, which I first formed in 1968, was driven by the enthusiasm of men, the new spirit that gripped the country and the support of Sheikh Zayed and Sheikh Rashid, who approved the strategy after reviewing it with me scores of times.

After the establishment of the Union on December 2nd, 1971, I began to manage the handover of responsibilities by the British forces, hoping to make the transition as smooth as possible. I knew the Royal Air Force Base in Sharjah very well. Both Royal Air Force personnel and an infantry battalion of about 2,500 people were based there. On December 22nd, the Trucial Oman Scouts became the Union Defence Force. The Scouts were originally established by Britain in 1951 to ensure security and stability in the area from Abu Dhabi to Ras Al Khaimah.

> # When my men were called to fight, I fought alongside them, making sure I was among the first to reach the battlefield and the last to leave

Its officers and men were initially members of the British Armed Forces who had served in India, some soldiers from the Arab Legion in Jordan, and our own Emirati citizens who had been trained by the British. The force included five infantry companies, a support corps, a wireless company, a training company, an engineering company, a medical company, a military band and a school for children.

This force formed the nucleus of our armed forces, which expanded to include the local defence forces established by the UAE rulers: the Abu Dhabi Defence Force, the Dubai Defence Force, the Ras Al Khaimah Mobile Force, the National Guard of Sharjah and the National Guard of Umm Al Quwain.

My first goal as Minister of Defence was to unify our armed forces before the start of 1976. I worked for a long time on the command structure and the five-year military strategy, and with God's help, I managed to adhere to the timeframe that I had set for myself.

I had a force capable of defending the homeland in the event of an attack. Now I needed to start implementing a full unification and integration programme.

I received full cooperation from the nation's leaders, especially Sheikh Zayed and Sheikh Rashid, to devise a strategy that would reflect the entire United Arab Emirates, and lead to the formation of a powerful army for our people. Because I invited these leaders to share their opinions, not only about the outcome but the process itself, I was blessed with their full support and encouragement.

During the development phase, I identified the equipment and technology that we needed and made sure to test and examine every piece of hardware required. I could gauge what would perform well in our desert, what would be effective and suitable for different terrains – vehicles, weapons and systems that could resist the harsh desert conditions to keep our men safe and constantly mobilised. The rulers could see that I had given my very best to accomplishing my mission, so they were certain – as was I – that the budget set was realistic and would not be wasted.

For me, establishing the Ministry of Defence was far more than simply laying the foundations for a new office building. I knew that institutionalising the ministry depended primarily on quickly establishing relationships and enduring networks. To achieve this quickly, I began to hold meetings with my counterparts, the defence ministers of other countries, and we had envoys travelling around the region on a daily basis. We sent groups to train with other militaries to understand them and build cooperation.

We also learned about the different strategic approaches and defence systems deployed in neighbouring countries such as Jordan, Sudan and Egypt. We sent officers to the United Kingdom, Italy and France. Thanks to my elite group of officers, we were able to achieve remarkable progress and I could delegate responsibilities to my strong team while I was working on developing the ministry.

Despite the pressure of this work, I made sure I did not miss a single morning's training in the yard with my men, because I was keen to follow developments carefully and to keep abreast of all events.

During the graduation of a military course

Working 19 hours a day was part of our normal life. During those days, I made my first equipment purchase as well. The process had to be transparent so that my men would see that we had chosen the best military kit available, which pleased everyone. Our Scorpion tanks were very suitable in terms of their light weight and the agility they offered in desert terrain. Bell helicopters arrived from Texas and Aermacchi training aircraft from Italy, all of which I inspected personally.

As exciting as those days were, they also involved many challenges and risks. When my men were called to fight, I fought alongside them, making sure I was among the first to reach the battlefield and the last to leave.

Emergencies we dealt with included armed conflicts between tribes, an attempted coup d'état involving the murder of Sharjah's ruler, attempted commercial plane hijackings, regional tensions and many ongoing threats to the emirates.

Throughout these turbulent times, we could see that we were on the right path, that our Union was taking root day by day, and that our armed forces were constantly evolving and improving their skills and capabilities.

Guided by the wisdom of Sheikh Zayed and Sheikh Rashid and fuelled by the efforts and loyalty of the armed forces, we were able to overcome all these threats to the infant state to reach the point where the United Arab Emirates had become one of the strongest forces in the Arab world.

30

The Ordeal of Flight 404

During the negotiations with Osamu Maruoka in 1973

The very first conversation I had with a terrorist was in July 1973. His name was Osamu Maruoka and he was one of the key figures of the Japanese Red Army (JRA), an organisation which aimed, among other things, to overthrow the Japanese monarchy and government. The JRA had established strong relationships with the Popular Front for the Liberation of Palestine (PFLP) in support of the Palestinian cause. In July 1973, Maruoka, with members of the PFLP, hijacked a Japan Airlines (JAL) aircraft with 118 passengers and threatened to blow up the plane, killing everyone on board.

How can any reasonable person ever come to an understanding with a group whose thinking is governed by that logic? Who would want to take the lives of the innocent to liberate others? They want to make a grand gesture of helping oppressed people through oppressing and killing others. They exploit the sympathy of some communities for a just cause, while recruiting members to terrorise other innocent groups of people. Contrary to their thinking, the very worst way to promote a worthy cause is for terrorists to adopt it as their personal struggle. If you want to hold back justice for a good cause, just let the terrorists act in your name and let them bring violence and misery to communities who otherwise enjoy safety.

For many decades, our region has suffered from this utterly self-defeating and oppressive thinking: that terror is a solution to injustice. Countries have lost thousands – even hundreds of thousands – of people to this philosophy of hatred. Many communities around the globe have lost decades of growth and development because of a terrorist ideology that begins with a just cause and ends with the utterly unjustified slaughter of innocent lives.

I was at a military base on July 20th, 1973, when my telephone rang. I was informed that JAL Flight 404, a Boeing 747-246B inbound for Tokyo with 123 passengers and 22 crew members on board, had been hijacked shortly after take-off from Amsterdam-Schiphol International Airport. The hijackers, led by Maruoka and including four PFLP members, were demanding permission to land at Dubai International Airport.

I immediately informed Sheikh Zayed and Sheikh Rashid of the situation and headed for the airport to make the necessary arrangements before the aircraft's arrival. I gave orders to evacuate the airfield and to direct all incoming aircraft to other airports nearby. My team and I were in position, waiting for the JAL airliner to enter the airspace of the United Arab Emirates and communicate with the air traffic control tower. We soon heard the pilots' voices and I gave permission for the hijacked plane to land on our nation's soil, in what was the first ever incident of its kind.

The plane touched down already in poor condition, as a grenade had exploded on board, killing one of the hijackers. Miraculously, the plane survived the explosion and arrived safely in the UAE. Upon landing, Maruoka's voice was heard over the radio, demanding to speak to one of the country's officials. I picked up the receiver and said, "Talk! I'm listening."

He asked me to introduce myself. After I did, he said, "So, you are an Arab, therefore you must support the Palestinian cause. It is your cause!" He informed me that they wanted to take refuge in the UAE.

I told him the passengers were tired of enduring this ordeal. They had done absolutely nothing wrong

Even over the radio, I could sense the tension and strain he was under. First, I asked him whether they had enough food and drink on board or needed more. He responded with great agitation, "Don't change the subject. We have explosives. We have weapons. We will kill all the passengers!"

I did my best to ease the tension and calmly discussed his demands. I told him that the Palestinian people's cause was indeed our cause, but I could not grant him safe passage. I could, however, assist him in any other matter. So he said, "Yes, we do have another demand." His demand was to release one of their detained comrades in Israel.

I asked him to be realistic. "Do you really think we even negotiate with Israel? We have no relationship with them." I said.

I told him I wished to speak with one of the Palestinian hijackers, hoping that I might convince him to act sensibly. I tried to engage in a conversation with one of the Palestinian leaders, but he was even louder and more agitated than his Japanese companion.

> A wise enemy is better than an ignorant and foolish ally. Perhaps our abundance of foolish allies has harmed many of our just causes

I went back to speaking with Maruoka, always in the same even tone of voice, explaining to him the contradiction between objecting to the Palestinian people's plight, while at the same time carrying out similar atrocities against other innocent people.

We maintained this back-and-forth for a while and, although I was able to gain his trust, I and everyone else knew that he was also now planning his next move. We understood each other and I was clear in my refusal to meet his demands.

The conversation lasted for many long hours extended over three days, during which Sheikh Zayed and Sheikh Rashid stayed informed, for they knew that I needed to be alone in dealing with the situation. We delivered food to the plane twice and noticed that things seemed peaceful on board. We did not see any evidence that anyone else had been hurt and the hijackers seemed to be calming down as well.

At dawn on the second day, Maruoka's voice resonated across the radio, saying, "Good morning. I hope you had a good sleep." He was deliberately mocking. He seemed to know that I had not slept.

I told him the passengers were tired of enduring this ordeal. They had done absolutely nothing wrong, and I asked him to release them. He responded tensely, threatening to blow up the plane. I replied that I understood his motives in supporting the people of Palestine, and that we appreciated it, but that he must be wise and patient. "This is not how we express our support for the Palestinian cause," I said. "We must all have sympathy for these innocent people. Please release them."

Sometimes he would calm down, before shouting again, "I have a lot of explosives! I can blow up this plane right now!"

On the third day, I told Maruoka, who by the sound of his voice was starting to become tired and worn down, that we agreed to refuel the plane and that he could fly it wherever he wished, but that we would not accept having the hijackers seek asylum in the United Arab Emirates. Indeed, once the plane was refuelled, he headed for Libya, where all of the passengers and flight attendants were released. The hijackers then blew up the plane at Benghazi Airport. Maruoka was not lying about the amount of explosives he had on board. I thank God that our negotiations gave him at least the good sense not to blow the plane up with any passengers on board. The entire incident was a valuable life lesson for me; a wise enemy is better than an ignorant and foolish ally. Perhaps our abundance of foolish allies in the Arab world has harmed many of our just causes.

31

A Coup in the Early Days of the Union

If you want to destroy a state from within, shake its political stability. If you want to change the narrative, to spread fear and redefine loyalties, then go after political stability. If you want to promote plotting and conspiracies and divide a society into factions, then target political stability. Stable rule, respect for the power of the state and upholding its constitution are all foundations of a sound polity. They are prerequisites to maintaining order and peaceful interaction between all elements of society.

The first attempt to shake the political stability of the United Arab Emirates was a coup d'état in the emirate of Sharjah, less than two months after the declaration of the Union. I was responsible for quelling the attempt. Sheikh Zayed was resolute when we talked about the attempted coup. He said to me, "Mohammed, resolve the matter quickly."

Sheikh Khalid bin Mohammed bin Saqr Al Qasimi had been the Ruler of Sharjah since 1965. He had played a crucial role in our work to found the Union, and he signed the Interim Constitution on December 2nd, 1971, making Sharjah part of the United Arab Emirates. It was inconceivable to allow anyone to threaten the stability and legitimate rule of one of our emirates.

The news travelled fast, but although I knew an attempted coup was taking place, I did not know who was behind it, which complicated matters. It was hard to correctly assess the situation because information was sketchy. I gave orders to cut off electricity to Sheikh Khalid's palace, where fighting was taking place, and then I called them directly. A guard answered the phone and I asked him who he was. "I am the guard of Sheikh Saqr bin Sultan, Ruler of Sharjah," he replied. With that, I knew who was leading the coup and informed Sheikh Zayed of the gravity of the situation.

Sheikh Saqr bin Sultan bin Saqr Al Qasimi, the former Ruler of Sharjah, was known for his support for Arab nationalist politics, so our main fear was that his motivation ran deeper than an internal dispute over governance. We were also afraid that he might have supporters and followers outside the country. Sheikh Zayed ordered me to take action swiftly, out of fear of any further ramifications and to prevent Sheikh Saqr from being able to acquire supplies from a third party.

I requested troops from Abu Dhabi in addition to mobilising resources from Dubai, for I did not know the size of force that supported Sheikh Saqr. The arrival of the units took time that I found I could not afford. All I could think about was the danger threatening the Union and the President's clear message that this coup d'état must not succeed.

I set off for Sheikh Khalid's palace along with two of my aides. I arrived at the palace and spoke with Sheikh Saqr over the telephone. My forces had not arrived yet, but I talked to him as if a large army was standing behind me, poised to storm the palace at any moment, leaving no room for escape. To this day, I cannot be certain whether that was actually a tactical error or inspired military strategy. All I know is that my instinct at the time told me that displays of confidence in such situations tend to shake your opponent and undermine their morale.

Sheikh Saqr and I began negotiations. I spoke from a position of strength and with full authority. I told him, "If Sheikh Khalid is well, I have a plane standing by to take you and whoever is with you to any country you want. But if Sheikh Khalid is hurt, I will turn you over to Sheikh Zayed who will do as he sees fit."

He fell silent for what seemed like eternity, then answered that Sheikh Khalid had been killed. His words made my blood boil. "Then you have five minutes to get out," I said. He and his son Sultan walked out with their hands by their sides, unlike those accompanying them, who came out with their hands above their heads. We stripped everyone of their arms. I had a cloth pulled across my face so that Sheikh Saqr would not know who I was as I advanced towards him. I was nervous about what he might have under his shirt, but he did not make any moves. He knew that there was no option but to surrender. He knew that the new state would not accept him after what he had done to his cousin, not to mention his efforts to derail the political stability of the United Arab Emirates. I saw a number of dead bodies scattered around the palace. I put him and his son in a car and sent them into custody until the President could issue a judgement in their regard. As for his supporters, I knew most of them and that they had been manipulated. I sent them back to their homes, resolving to call them back at a later time. I was keen to put an end to the matter as swiftly as possible. Sheikh Zayed was closely following the developments of this coup, which – he constantly stressed during his calls – must not succeed.

After the passing of Sheikh Khalid, may he rest in peace, his brother Sheikh Dr Sultan bin Mohammed Al Qasimi took over as Ruler of Sharjah and to this day continues to lead the flourishing emirate in prosperity and stability.

The coup was an incredibly difficult experience to undergo at the very start of our Union. Following these events, I felt that the Union was still a newborn and that many eyed it with ambition and greed. I knew that protecting it would not be an easy task, and I understood that its stability was more prone to threats from the inside than from enemies on the outside. I was on constant guard for a repeat of something of this nature, treating any possible threat with extreme caution. Every time the telephone rang, I would jump up and brace myself for the worst. I do not remember ever answering the telephone while seated throughout all those years.

Once the coup d'état was over, I met with Sheikh Zayed in his car. He handed me some dates and then a cup of coffee, looking at me with pride and appreciation, a look that said, "Mohammed, you are the man of the moment!" This simple but heartfelt gesture was one of the greatest rewards I have ever received in my life.

32

Terrorism Across Borders

Lufthansa Flight 181 in 1977

The worst thing that could ever happen to a nation is to be dragged into a crisis or conflict in which it has no part. One of the ultimate challenges that can ever face someone like myself, in charge of national security, is to discover that the unwelcome scourge of terrorism has crossed into your country, requiring action to avoid the loss of innocent lives.

In 1977, as the shadow of terrorism darkened the world's skies, anxiety became my constant companion. I remember I often experienced heartburn and an acid taste in my throat due to the constant rush of adrenaline.

During an early morning meeting at the Ministry of Defence, I was briefed on the unfolding events of a hijacked aircraft, a Lufthansa Boeing 737, carrying 91 people on board including the flight crew. Lufthansa Flight 181 was heading from Palma de Mallorca, Spain, to Frankfurt, Germany, when it was hijacked by members of the Popular Front for the Liberation of Palestine (PFLP), who demanded the release of their imprisoned comrades in West Germany.

This story captured my full attention and I followed the breaking news coming from on board the plane. For some reason, I had an acute presentiment that this drama was about to involve the UAE. I learned that the hijackers had headed for Larnaca in Cyprus and then on to Bahrain. At that moment, I realised for sure that we needed to prepare ourselves to support our Bahraini brothers. While that would have been reason enough to follow the progress of the hijacked plane as it flew towards the Gulf, the real reasons for my premonitions became clear, for after the plane refuelled in Bahrain, it headed for Dubai.

"Eighty-six passengers. Five flight crew. Ninety-one souls." This was all that was going through my mind at that moment.

I rushed to the door and ordered my men, "Tell the President! Tell Sheikh Rashid!" The phrase 'Ninety-one passengers and crew' haunted me. I headed to the airport at lightning speed. I spent 60 minutes preparing my men to deal with the situation; the time it takes to get from Bahrain to Dubai. Sixty. Ninety-one. These numbers kept running through my head until I reached the air traffic control tower.

Once inside the tower, I quickly called Sheikh Zayed and my father. I needed more time. I needed more than just a single hour to put together medical teams and position the snipers and armoured cars where the hijackers could not see them. After learning about the situation, Sheikh Zayed answered my call within seconds and went straight to the point, "Mohammed, tell me what you need."

I asked him, as the Supreme Commander of the Armed Forces, for his permission to communicate with the aircraft and authorise it to land. Our normal policy was not to allow any hijacked aircraft to land on our territory. I received his approval, as he was certain that I would stay in control of the situation.

When everything was set, I addressed the aircraft from the air traffic control tower, "Lufthansa Flight 181, we authorise you to land on our territory. You can now land at Dubai." I heard the voice of the pilot respond and tried to imagine the mood in the cockpit as we watched the Boeing 737 land on the runway. We knew we were in for an ordeal.

After the plane landed, one of the hijackers took over the microphone, his voice booming through the control tower. I remained calm so that I could hear him clearly and appraise his frame of mind. The passengers' lives seemed closer to being rescued. I listened to his demands, then I agreed to deliver food and water to the plane.

I maintained communications with the hijacker and did not need a team of psychoanalysts to assess the state of the man before me. It was clear that he was mentally disturbed and unbalanced. I realised that the lives of the passengers were at the mercy of a person who might have a breakdown at any moment. He spoke very quickly and unclearly about his imperialist enemies who ruled the world. The hijackers had demanded the release of their comrades, members of the left-wing Baader-Meinhof group – also known as the Red Army Faction – who were serving lengthy prison sentences in Germany.

For 48 hours, I continued to speak with a man who followed no discernible logic. He talked about his family and many different topics that had no common thread. I repeatedly asked him to surrender, but he refused. I did not respond to every demand he made, but would immediately calm him down once he started threatening to kill the passengers. I had to cut off communication for a short while to speak with German government officials, and we delivered necessary food and other supplies to the plane. We needed to get close to the plane in order to help the passengers and crew.

I thought about their families and imagined how I would feel if a member of my family were held hostage on this plane. I knew that the slightest wrong move could lead to loss of life. The best way was to try to wait them out, negotiate and convince the hijackers that they would not get what they wanted and that they must surrender.

I was sure that the terrorists would ask for more fuel once they knew that the UAE would not offer them asylum in exchange for the lives of the passengers. After the 48 hours of discussions with that man, I got to know him very well, more than many people who have lived together a long time may know each other!

To prevent the hijackers from making good on their threat to kill the passengers one by one, every ten minutes, until the plane took off, we agreed to supply the plane with fuel. Finally fuelled and ready, the plane took off. My heart went too, along with those 91 souls.

When the plane arrived in Aden, one of the hijackers shot the captain, Jürgen Schumann, and threw his body on the runway in an attempt to force authorities to meet their demands. As time went on, I continued to hear his voice every time I closed my eyes. I was the last person he talked to before he flew out of Dubai. When the plane took off from the runway and was high in the sky, I said, "May God protect you, captain." I heard him click his microphone, indicating that he had heard my prayer for his safety.

After the captain was killed, the hijackers' demands were met; the aircraft took on more fuel in Aden and headed to Mogadishu, Somalia. I prayed to God to help the passengers during those difficult hours, and felt immense relief when I heard that a German anti-terrorism unit had successfully stormed the plane, freeing the passengers after killing three of the hijackers and arresting the fourth, who was a woman. None of the passengers, who had been my sole focus for all that time on the tarmac, were killed. The remaining crew members were not hurt. But that brave captain had lost his life.

That October seemed to stretch out endlessly amid increasing international tensions, culminating in the loss of one more innocent soul to terrorism – and this time in the land of the United Arab Emirates. On that day, I had attended meetings in Abu Dhabi with the Syrian Foreign Minister, Abdul Halim Khaddam. It was a busy time, filled with discussions about the situation in the region. As I got into my car to return to Dubai, I looked back on the talks with worry. I felt the chill of October all around me. I stopped my car on the side of the road to answer an emergency call dispatched over the radio. I picked up the receiver and heard shocking news.

Abdul Halim Khaddam had been on his way to Abu Dhabi International Airport when he was targeted by a hitman. Instead, the bullets had hit Saif bin Ghobash, the United Arab Emirates' Minister of State for Foreign Affairs, who was accompanying him. It was hard for me to imagine that he had been so full of life just a few moments before. He died while giving his best to his country and yet had so much more to offer. I wondered, "How could anyone be so cruel and take a life so easily?"

At that moment, because I despise killing and unjustified violence, I promised myself I would make this country a safe and peaceful place for every citizen, resident and visitor. I started to view any violence taking place inside our borders as if it were an act carried out against each and every one of us and against me personally.

33

Mission Accomplished

With Sheikh Zayed bin Sultan honouring armed forces personnel

One of the greatest milestones in my life, one of the proudest days of my journey and also one of my greatest challenges, took place on May 6th, 1976, which witnessed the official unification of the UAE's Armed Forces.

It was a sensitive task on a national level, but an essential one. It was difficult, but the soldiers and officers of the United Arab Emirates made it achievable. The spirit of the Union ran through their veins. Day after day, they saw crises and wars ravaging the region, and this made them fear for their homeland, which had no powerful, unified force. Finally they witnessed the fruits of hard work and perseverance.

Each emirate possessed its own local defence force. However, as a philosopher once said, "All power is weak unless united." This belief was instilled in the soul of every Emirati and conscience of every ruler, as well as in the hearts of all the officers and soldiers who pledged to die for their homeland.

I always used to tell my companions, "The Union is like a tree; the nation represents its soil, the sacrifices we make are its water and the humans are its fruit. The trunk of that tree is its forces and army." The trunk must never be weak or disjointed. The trunk must be a strong, solid one that can support the tree and protect it from storms. I used to say, "Our success resides in being together, our progress resides in working together. We must always stay together for the future to be our ally. Everything will be easy, if we stick together. Alone we can do just a little, but together we can do so much more."

We only had five years to unify our armed forces. During the first term of the newly formed federal government, we devised a structure and strategy to achieve that goal. The plan was adopted by Sheikh Zayed, Sheikh Rashid and all the other rulers, while all military units were equally committed to it.

Our steps were gradual, but serious and confident, towards our ultimate goal. In 1974, in my capacity as Minister of Defence, I issued a decree that changed the name of the Union Defence Force to the United Arab Emirates Armed Forces and gave the force a new emblem and flag. I maintained the same tasks, duties, organisation and human resources grades. I also maintained the same forces, companies and training sites. The steps we took reflected the final vision we must achieve in just two years. The force consisted of seven infantry companies, as well as a Scorpion light tank regiment, a support company, a paratroop company and a cadet company, under my direct supervision. Additionally, the individual emirates' local defence forces remained in place.

We had come a long way in developing our combat formations, fire support and administrative systems, while adhering to a combat ethos based on self-defence and protection of the country's sovereignty. The changes occurring around us, especially the Arab-Israeli conflict, imposed an atmosphere of permanent instability in the region. I constantly pushed for the formation of a new Arab force that would constitute a barrier for the country, a support for our friends and a deterrent against enemies lying in wait.

Finally, on May 6th, 1976, came the historic event that I felt fulfilled my promise to Sheikh Zayed and my father. I felt that our mission had been accomplished, that our souls had been comforted and that

On May 6th, 1976, came the
historic event. I felt that our
mission had been accomplished,
that our souls had been comforted
and that the real force of our
nation was now in place

With Sheikh Zayed bin Sultan

the real force of our nation was now in place. On that day, the Federal Supreme Council issued a decree to unify the armed forces in Bu Mraikha, Abu Dhabi, under the leadership of the late Sheikh Zayed bin Sultan Al Nahyan. In this respect, a statement was made by the Supreme Defence Council, which said:

> "As part of our continuous endeavours to support the Union, to unify its pillars and to strengthen its stability, security and progress; and in the belief that historical responsibility obliges us to work with altruism to dismantle all the barriers hindering communication, and to ensure the full integration of State institutions; and in response to the desire of Their Highnesses, the members of the Federal Supreme Council, to work towards achieving the hopes and aspirations of the people, the armed forces have been united under one flag and command to serve as a strong line of defence protecting our homeland, and to play its role as a force protecting Arabs."

On that day, Sheikh Zayed, President of the United Arab Emirates, may God have mercy upon his soul, became the Supreme Commander of the United Arab Emirates Armed Forces. His Highness Sheikh Khalifa bin Zayed Al Nahyan was elected Deputy Supreme Commander of the United Arab Emirates Armed Forces, and I was ratified as Minister of Defence. A Chief of Staff of the Armed Forces was elected, along with three other assistants. Another decree was issued by the President of the Supreme Defence Council, Sheikh Zayed, stipulating the unification of land, sea and air forces under one central command, called the General Command of the United Arab Emirates Armed Forces.

The decision also included the establishment of three military zones, namely: The Northern Military Zone (formerly known as the Ras Al Khaimah Mobile Force), the Western Military Zone (formerly known as the Abu Dhabi Defence Force), and the Central Military Zone (formerly known as the Dubai Defence Force).

The decision also established the Yarmuk Brigade, including all of the Union Defence Force, the National Guard of Sharjah and the National Guard of Umm Al Quwain, as well as the Air Force Command and Naval Force Command. At the same time, we created several training institutes such as the Zayed Military College, as well as dedicated training establishments for infantry, paratroopers, amour and artillery. The military flag, emblem, uniform and flags of the commanders were unified, and proudly worn, as well.

The unification was then complete, and I had fulfilled the mission I started back in 1968; three years before the Union's inception, when Sheikh Rashid told me, "We shall declare the formation of the Union, and you shall be responsible for its protection."

I never felt at peace until 1976 when all the forces were united under one flag, one emblem and one wise leader, Sheikh Zayed bin Sultan Al Nahyan. On that day, I felt that I had fulfilled my promise to build a strong force, capable of protecting our country. On that day, I felt that I, along with my fellow soldiers, had succeeded in contributing to the establishment of the solid foundations of a strong, sovereign state that would never be stopped by internal or external threats from realising its dreams and aspirations and continuing its march to progress.

34

Between War & Peace

With my father Sheikh Rashid bin Saeed Al Maktoum

States, like individuals, face difficult decisions, such as choosing between economic and military development, between investing resources into building things up or burning them down, between war and peace.

There are some specific choices that come to mind when I recall the year 1979. That year, I saw the decisions that we were making in my country and those being made in other countries in the region. Today, 40 years later, we see the results quite clearly.

A pivotal year in Dubai's history, 1979 saw the launch of three of the emirate's largest projects. The first was Jebel Ali Port, and the second was the aluminium smelter established by Dubai Aluminium Company (DUBAL) with an initial annual capacity of 135,000 tonnes. The third major project that began that year was the Dubai International Trade Centre (now known as the Dubai World Trade Centre), which was the tallest building in the Middle East and one of the largest buildings in the world at the time.

That year, we finally started to feel like we were making giant strides, that our battle to build our nation was beginning to bear fruit and that the world was starting to know who we were. We began to realise that our seemingly boundless ambition could be realised and that no power could stand in our way. Our hopes and dreams soared – the sky really was the limit.

However, 1979 also witnessed a revolution and change of regime in Iran, and Saddam Hussein's rise to power in Iraq. We also saw the slide towards all-out confrontation between Iraq and Iran, a war that would have a significant impact on all our futures.

By late 1979 and early 1980, relations between the two states with the largest populations and most powerful armies in the region had reached boiling point. This was one of the most painful times in my life because I realised we were heading into a tunnel, not knowing how or when we would ever emerge.

As our two biggest neighbours shaped up for a clash, my own responsibilities increased. In addition to heading the Ministry of Defence, I was called on to assist Sheikh Zayed in his mediation efforts. I was able to learn valuable diplomatic lessons, accompanying him on trips or representing him in summit meetings to try to avert the conflict.

By August 1980, it was becoming clear that diplomacy had failed in avoiding war, leaving no choice but to prepare myself for a conflict on our borders, both personally and in my position as Minister of Defence. On September 4th, 1980, Iraq accused Iran of bombing border towns, including Khanaqin and Mandali. On September 22nd, the Iran-Iraq War broke out, a conflict that was to last for eight devastating years. We remained neutral but never idle, launching the largest construction phase in our country, enabling us to take major strides in development.

One unexpected result of the Iran-Iraq war was to push the Gulf states to think collectively about protecting themselves and achieving economic growth. The establishment of the Gulf Cooperation Council (GCC) as a regional political and economic organisation was tabled. As a strong supporter of federalism, I was very enthusiastic about the idea and resolved to help my colleagues in the GCC realise our aspiration to defend the Gulf region through cooperation. On May 25th, 1981, the GCC was formally established. That same month, I sat proudly behind Sheikh Zayed as he inaugurated the Foundation Summit in Abu Dhabi. This is what I had dreamed of: the type of cooperative initiative that would positively affect the region as a whole.

I hope that leaders of all Arab countries would consider such a model of cooperation among themselves to achieve peace and serve their peoples. It is certainly achievable; I have experienced it twice in my

Queen Elizabeth at the opening of the Dubai Aluminium Company (DUBAL) in 1979

life: the Union of the United Arab Emirates and the establishment of the Gulf Cooperation Council.

Although we remained neutral in the war, we were forced to protect our oil installations in the Gulf, as the blue waters of our seas became the arena for the so-called 'tanker war', when Iraqi and Iranian forces attempted to cut off oil supplies and force the West to intervene. The targeting extended even to commercial vessels of other countries who were not party to the war.

We could not stand idly by as our own tankers were attacked. This prompted the deployment of our own maritime and air forces. In October 1983, we organised our first joint exercises with the Omani, Saudi and Bahraini armed forces, as well as Kuwait and Qatar under Operation Peninsula Shield.

During the mid 1980s, tankers belonging to many neighbouring countries were bombed in the waters of the Arabian Gulf, leading to the death of employees and workers and affecting the entire maritime sector throughout the region.

To avoid further damage, we pulled some of our ships into our territorial waters. I will never forget the efforts made by Sheikh Zayed during the war to lay the foundations for negotiations in the hope of achieving peace. At the time, my world was all about military matters and security concerns and my work was focused on protecting my homeland, as the war in the region became part of a conflict between major powers, especially after the United States joined the tanker war.

In July 1988, the American warship *USS Vincennes* mistakenly fired two missiles at an Iranian Airlines Airbus 320 heading for Dubai; killing all 290 passengers on board. Two weeks after the tragic incident, Iran officially announced its acceptance of United Nations Security Council Resolution 598, which called for an immediate end to the Iran-Iraq War.

Grinding on for almost a decade, the war eventually ended – but at a hideous cost of more than a million deaths and over a trillion dollars' worth of losses.

There were no winners in that war, and even today we still don't fully understand why it started.

What we do know is that DUBAL, after its merger with Emirates Aluminium (EMAL), has become the world's fifth largest aluminium producer. Jebel Ali Port has a free zone that is home to more than 7,000 companies, and we have successfully scaled up our experience worldwide, managing some 80 ports across the globe today.

As for the Dubai World Trade Centre, it is now the largest exhibition centre in the region, drawing more than three million business people, experts and specialists every year to roughly 500 world-class events. The Sheikh Zayed Road, which began with a single tower, is now flanked by more skyscrapers than any other road in the Middle East. So, after some 40 years – a mere blink of an eye in the life of a nation – one can see the results of choices made between war and peace, between risking it all for development or for politics.

35

Destination
Dubai

An aerial view of Dubai

Visions are passed down through generations, our minds conceive and share new ideas and our parents pass their characteristics on to us. The environment we live in also influences our specific vision for the future. Today, as I trace the development of Dubai and its people, these thoughts run through my mind.

My grandfather, Sheikh Saeed bin Maktoum, was a firm believer in openness to the world and the liberalisation of the economy. He succeeded in lifting the depression that hit Dubai after the collapse of the pearl trade in the 1930s, by calling on merchants to establish their businesses around the city's creekside port.

Then came my father, Sheikh Rashid, who moved further along his own father's path, taking Dubai to new heights. My father learned from my grandfather that Dubai's economic lifeblood, the qualities that make it special and unique are its openness to the world and its relations with other people across the globe. This is especially significant when it comes to business. He borrowed money and invested in expanding the Creek and building Port Rashid – the largest port in the region at the time. He then built the colossal Jebel Ali Port, redefining imagination. From the late 1950s, my father struggled to build an international airport for Dubai. Initially, Britain tried to prevent him from doing so, but he prevailed and managed to bring his dream to life. Deep down in his heart, it was a passion that he inherited from my grandfather: that Dubai had to embrace the world and establish unbreakable global ties.

I was about ten years old when I first understood that we, in Dubai, had the potential to become a global city capable of receiving businesses and visitors from all over the world. At the time, this was

I knew he was about to hear something wholly different from what he expected. He pulled his chair back, took out his pipe and gave me his full attention

just a vague emotion I felt while I stood bewildered at London's Heathrow Airport, when I first visited Britain. I saw the long queues of visitors and business people arriving and departing, and scores of aircraft landing and releasing the multitudes of people coming to London, or travelling onwards to different continents, carrying with them British business and culture. That was in 1959, when my father was visiting the British capital to try to persuade the Prime Minister at the time, Harold Macmillan, to allow Dubai to build an airport. On that day I was merely dreaming that we would have our own airport, but as the years passed that dream became reality and I began working on the political and military aspects of our new Union, as we began to build a unified nation. Throughout that time, one conviction remained in my mind: the one I had inherited, that our future lay in making Dubai a global destination; but it wasn't easy.

A memorable instance of the early struggles we faced is when my father asked the British Overseas Airways Corporation (BOAC), to recognise the inauguration of Dubai Airport with regular flights to Mumbai (or Bombay as it was then known). BOAC refused giving the excuse that their studies found scarce demand for seats on that route. My father answered: "Make the link between Dubai and Bombay and I shall cover the cost of any vacant seats on the flight."

BOAC agreed, and began operating a regular flight. The plan worked, with one airline after another adding flights to and from Dubai, until 15 operators were linking us to 42 destinations across the Middle East and Europe. By the late 1970s, the success of these early initiatives had shaped a clear overall vision in my mind. One evening, I was talking with my father, and I told him that we needed to develop our aviation sector and make it bigger, invest differently in our airport, and begin marketing Dubai in a new way.

Palm Jumeirah, Dubai

My father looked me in the eyes. He saw how serious I was and challenged me: "Give me your plan within two days."

Two days later, I entered his office knowing he was about to hear something wholly different from what he expected. I laid my papers before him and smiled. He smiled too, in anticipation, as he pulled his chair back, took out his pipe, and gave me his full attention. I presented to him a strategy that I had named 'Destination Dubai'. It did not involve merely developing the airport, but the whole city as a destination. I spoke to him about expanding the airport, and about an open skies policy to encourage airlines to service Dubai, as well as marketing campaigns to promote the city, the building of new hotels in the emirate, and the organisation of major events like horse championships to attract people. I spoke to him about the income that would be generated by all of this. We did not speak for long, but

Towers in Dubai Marina

our thoughts were very focused and full of ambition. My ambitions, my ideas and my impulsiveness may even have sounded crazy at the time. I finished talking, and I waited for him to answer. His reply was a big smile and just one word, "*Namus*", which in our culture means 'fine'. In short, he was satisfied with everything that I had presented to him. From that day, I was appointed to take charge of all issues related to trade, tourism, marketing and the development of aviation in Dubai. We began the journey then and we continue travelling to this day.

During the early 1980s, for example, Dubai International Airport had just a few small stores selling food, drink, magazines and other travellers' needs. We heard about Shannon International Airport in Ireland, where the first duty-free area was established. We asked for a team from there to help us develop a duty-free area in our airport. I remember the plan that one of our young men, Mohi-Din BinHendi, put together for the establishment of Dubai's duty-free area in 1983. I felt he was being overly cautious with his proposals. I said to him, "Double the area." And so we inaugurated the duty-free zone, six months later. Today, Dubai Duty Free is one of the largest in the world, serving around 90 million travellers every year and accounting for five per cent of all global duty free sales.

A few years ago, British newspapers carried the story that Dubai International Airport had surpassed London Heathrow as the busiest airport in the world. As I read those headlines, I remembered standing in awe, more than 50 years ago, at Heathrow Airport, and said to myself, "Glory be to God!"

36

Cooperation

A meeting of the Gulf Cooperation Council

I was one of the most optimistic people regarding the Gulf Cooperation Council (GCC), when it was established, because I knew that power does not lie in division but in pooling and sharing forces. Cooperating would make us stronger, richer and more influential than any other country in the region. I knew that the collective potential of all the Gulf states was massive, with vast wealth, culturally connected communities, shared hopes and fears and stable governments. We had no excuses.

On the sidelines of one of the GCC's meetings during the early 1980s, while the ministers discussed the headline crises and challenges, I made a suggestion. By then I was in my mid 30s. I was the youngest person in the meeting, and certainly the most bored by all the seemingly endless political talk. I said to them, "Why don't we try to develop the region, especially Dubai, as a tourist destination to attract people from all over the world?"

I felt them all turn to look in my direction. Silence prevailed for a few seconds, before one of the older foreign affairs ministers burst out laughing. He said, "What will the tourists find in Dubai? Who is going to come and visit a desert? Who is going to come to the heat and humidity of Dubai?" Then the rest joined in his laughter.

He put on an 'expert' tone of voice and continued, "Sheikh Mohammed, what is the cultural heritage that the tourists will see? What are the sites that they will visit? Sands behind them, the sea in front of them, and the sun above their heads?"

I did not feel like arguing with him, especially after he refused even to hear the details of my suggestion. His comments only made me more determined and convinced of the project and the plan going through my mind. I felt sad because we were not making good use of our wealth, we had no faith in the ideas of youth, and we were not willing to try anything new or different. I wish the cooperation had been in areas other than politics and military affairs, despite their importance at the time.

Sometimes I think that we need to reconsider our cooperation mechanisms in the Arab world, whether through the GCC or the Arab League, and rethink its fundamental structures and modes of operation. These mechanisms are managed by politicians, mainly ministers of foreign affairs, who are primarily concerned with firefighting political crises and therefore overlook longer-term opportunities and agendas.

I was constantly asking myself what would happen if these discussions took place among managers and leaders interested in development? What if they were mandated to serve their nations by developing new infrastructure for the benefit of all Arab peoples? What if their priority was investment to improve living conditions in the Arab world, establishing investment channels, building enterprises and partnerships and advancing science, technology, and research and development?

The Arab League is 70 years old. What if we had started all this 70 years ago? Where would we be today? Maybe the time has come for these mechanisms to be overseen by leaders, managers, businessmen, heads of industry and entrepreneurs instead of foreign ministers. Well, why not?

> We were not making good use of our wealth, we had no faith in the ideas of youth, and we were not willing to try anything new or different

Shortly after the answer from my friend, the Minister of Foreign Affairs, I was driving my car on a hot August day in Dubai. I saw a foreign family walking on the beach around noon. I offered them water, then asked them, what were they doing in Dubai? To which they replied, "We are tourists. We have come from Germany looking for the sun."

Their answer confirmed what I had long believed. Now I was fully convinced, and my faith soared. I knew that we were sitting on tourist gold: sun, sea and white sands. We could offer a safe and secure environment with glorious attractions, luxurious hotels and superb services.

We launched tourism campaigns, which attracted millions of visitors. I knew that the key to strengthening our tourism sector was our airport, and that more airlines had to be encouraged to use it. At that time, there were 40 airlines using Dubai International Airport, and

Maybe the time has come for these mechanisms to be overseen by leaders, managers, businessmen, heads of industry and entrepreneurs instead of foreign ministers

the open skies policy we adopted went on to attract even more. The tourism sector in Dubai went through distinct phases of development. The sector was totally new to us. But we learned, and we benefitted from the experiences of others and, as always, we took many developmental risks. We invested heavily in order to attract tourists, by building visitor and entertainment facilities, huge malls, state-of-the art facilities and infrastructure. Many of our friends asked who we were building it for, as we didn't have many tourists.

My answer to them was, "Build it and they will come."

They used to say to me, "Logically, it's demand before supply, you must have demand first, and then invest in the supply."

I always replied, "This theory could be true, but we know best how to develop our country."

A meeting of the Gulf Cooperation Council

Today, according to the United Nations' International Tourism Agency, the tourism sector in Dubai accounts for about a third of all the revenues from international tourism in the Middle East, with Dubai's share of tourism income reaching around 31 per cent, soaring to AED 77 billion ($21 billion) in 2017.

Some 16 million international tourists visited Dubai in 2017 and we are planning to welcome approximately 20 million tourists in 2020, the year Dubai hosts the World Expo.

Sometimes I wonder what would have been the outcome if we had cooperated with our brothers in the GCC in developing our tourism sectors together back in the 1980s? Would we have been more successful than we are now? Or would we have remained mired in endless feasibility studies until today? This is a question that I direct to their Excellencies the GCC Ministers of Foreign Affairs.

37

An Airline Company in Dubai

With Airbus CEO Stewart Wheeler unveiling an aircraft for Emirates in 1988

During my life, I have been through many adventures. I established companies without any previous experience. I ventured into new arenas I had no idea about, and I made decisions that no one had made before me, as far as I knew. But I did all of this based on very solid principles that I inherited from my forefathers, the principles related to the ruling of Dubai. These principles are based on openness to the world, equality for all, the rule of law, fair competition, the creation of opportunities for everyone to work, invest and be creative, and the right of every entrepreneur to compete fairly with every other, even if the latter was a ruler or the government. These are solid principles that have shown their worth over generations.

During the late 1970s, we launched the open skies policy for Dubai Airport in order to attract more airline companies. We were clear; any company in the world has the right to book any number of landing slots at Dubai Airport.

Our objective for adopting an open skies policy was to enhance our competitiveness and open up new sectors for our economy. However, this was not well received by some airlines, who were enjoying protection from their host countries.

Gulf Air, supported by some of the Gulf Cooperation Council (GCC) countries, was operating several regional flights to Dubai. They began to worry that they were merely feeding their passengers to international competitors for more lucrative long-haul flights. In 1983, there was a conflict between Gulf Air and Pakistan International Airlines (PIA) regarding landing rights. This caused Gulf Air to put pressure on a number of operators in the Gulf to stop supporting PIA.

The problems involving Gulf Air in Dubai Airport increased, until the airline blatantly demanded that we suspend the open skies policy in order to protect their share of the market. They warned us that we had a few weeks to submit to their terms, or they would withdraw from Dubai, which apparently meant that we would lose 70 per cent of the airport's traffic. The company thought it had the upper hand in this situation, and that it had the strength to force us to cave in to its ultimatum.

During a series of extremely tense meetings, I repeated that our open skies policy was not negotiable and explained to them over and over again that competition was necessary and at the core of our approach: that we were not going to put any limits on our airspace. We reached a standoff and Gulf Air responded by reducing its flights to Dubai.

I hate conflict because it is neither a smart nor civilised way to resolve problems. But, if the other party refuses to act in a civilised manner, then I am forced to act decisively.

In 1984, I invited the Director of the airline services company in Dubai, Maurice Flanagan, to my office to consult with him about a dream I have always had: the establishment of an airline for Dubai.

The airline would not be run by the government, but privately, unlike the airlines of all other Arab countries. The company would operate in line with private sector systems and would have total financial independence and sustainability. Flanagan was an expert in the airline business, as he had started his career with the British Overseas Airways Corporation (BOAC), following service with the

'I shall call it Emirates Airline,' I said, and I ordered that they put the flag of the United Arab Emirates on the tail of the aircraft

Royal Air Force. He was a member of the Senior Management of British Airways.

Flanagan said to me, "Your Highness, I can prepare an urgent study about that." I asked him to do just that, and quickly. Then I requested an independent study in order to be sure of the company's feasibility plan. Flanagan put together a team of ten managers and came back with a clear strategy.

The team made several suggestions including a name for this new airline. They suggested 'Dubai Airlines'.

"I shall call it Emirates Airline," I said, and I ordered that they put the flag of the United Arab Emirates on the tail of the aircraft.

"How much do you need to launch this new airline company?" I asked the team.

They said it would cost $10 million. My answer to them was: "Fine, but I shall not pay an extra cent."

From the day I made that decision, we had six months to announce the launch of the new airline. We leased two aircraft from PIA and we began to re-equip them in line with the new airline's brand and service offering. While we were preparing to launch, the team came to me and asked, "Can we get protection against the competition?"

My answer was clear, "No. The open skies policy will remain and it shall apply to us like it applies to everyone else."

I asked Sheikh Ahmed Bin Saeed Al Maktoum, who was a few years younger than me and had recently graduated from university in the United States, to preside over the new airline.

With very little time until the date of launch, Sheikh Ahmed and his team worked extremely hard, during weekends, and often during the night, in order to establish a superior offering to passengers. I took part in several meetings, and was constantly asking about their plans, and picking their brains.

Emirates Airline was to have four routes on launch: Karachi, Bombay, Delhi and Kuwait. Because of time pressure, we never let up, we never slowed down. It was obvious to me that Dubai would count on its skies in the same way it counts on its seas.

On October 25th, 1985, I was with my brother, Sheikh Maktoum, travelling on Emirates Airline's first flight to Karachi. We were very

With Sheikh Ahmed bin Saeed and Maurice Flanagan in an Emirates aircraft in 1992

enthusiastic even though everyone was exhausted from the stress of bringing the new airline into operation on schedule. I knew this was just the start of a long and difficult journey.

Today, Emirates Airline has won many international prizes as the best carrier and it has a long and profitable history spanning over 30 years. Total revenues in 2018 were about $28 billion and it carries about 60 million travellers every year with its fleet of 260 wide-bodied aircraft, employing some 100,000 staff.

Sometimes companies destroy themselves through fear of competition, leading to the creation of a competitor that will go on to eliminate them.

38

Bringing Dreams
to Reality

Jebel Ali Port

Steve Jobs, the founder of Apple, once said, "You can't connect the dots looking forward; you can only connect them looking backwards."

One morning during the mid 1970s, Neville Allen, who came to Dubai in 1958 as a representative of Sir William Halcrow and Partners, was awakened at 5am to the sound of his phone ringing. A voice at the other end informed him that the Ruler of Dubai wished to see him in the Jebel Ali area immediately.

Allen was a little upset with this unexpected and peremptory demand, but hurried to the specified rendezvous on a small hill where he found Sheikh Rashid bin Saeed waiting for him. Sheikh Rashid pointed to the coast and said, "I want to build a new port here."

In his usual manner, the Sheikh explained his idea and then asked how much the project was likely to cost. Allen gave him an estimate, and then inquired when the work should begin. Sheikh Rashid replied, "Immediately!"

We had previously inaugurated Port Rashid, and massive expansion works were underway to make it the largest port in the Middle East, with 35 berths.

And yet, only 35 kilometres away from the centre of Dubai, the Ruler wanted to build a port that was to be the largest, man-made port in the world, Jebel Ali Port. The cost was immense.

Some businessmen asked me to talk to him and discourage him. But he was very clear and wholly determined: "I shall build a project for you now that you will not be able to afford later."

Being alongside Sheikh Rashid while he worked and undertook projects gave me a new perspective and changed the way I think. He had exceptional vision, which gave you the feeling that you could, at times, bend the laws of logic to achieve the seemingly impossible.

Some years later, I was put in charge of business affairs, the ports, tourism and aviation in Dubai. The ball was in my court to continue bending the rules of logic to launch new daring dreams.

The year 1985 was different. I began to form two different dreams. The first was Emirates Airline, and the second was a free zone annexed to the port – a first of its kind in the region: a duty-free zone in Jebel Ali Port that would be a commercial and industrial region within which international companies could enjoy total ownership while receiving customs exemptions for all the goods they imported; goods that would go on to be re-exported through the huge port that Sheikh Rashid had built.

The prevailing commercial logic was that Dubai's revenues from customs fees formed one of the main pillars of its revenues – a fundamental principle that Sheikh Saeed and Sheikh Rashid instilled into me. Now we were building a duty-free zone that would allow businesses to import whatever they needed through Dubai without paying customs fees. True, we would lose customs revenue but we would gain much more from inward investment and increased trade.

I sent out a team to several countries to study this issue from all angles. Their findings were positive. We went ahead and launched the free trade zone. Within days, we had received some 300 requests

> Being alongside Sheikh Rashid while he worked gave you the feeling that you could bend the laws of logic to achieve the seemingly impossible

from companies wishing to locate there. I was very proud of the team led by Sultan bin Sulayem, his enthusiasm reflected my own and he led one of the most successful projects in Dubai.

In 1991, I ordered the merger of the administration functions of both our ports, at Jebel Ali and Port Rashid, under the banner of what would become The Dubai Ports Authority. This would create a stronger and more experienced administration. We acquired extensive experience over the years, enabling us to win contracts to build and run ports abroad. As Dubai Ports International expanded its operations managing overseas ports, it made sense to merge it with Dubai Ports Authority to form DP World.

Our dreams grew, and Emirates Airline grew with them, as did Dubai's airport, by now handling some 90 million passengers every year. DP World also grew to handle about 90 million container movements annually. I cannot account for the coincidence between

DP World

these two figures. Maybe we can explain it by looking back, as Steve Jobs said. Is the fact that they were launched during the same year relevant? Maybe it is relevant that I stood with my father 45 years ago atop that hill in Jebel Ali to plan the port. My father and I, two of us for 45 years, makes 90. But then, I do not really believe in coincidences.

In 2010, I launched an even more ambitious dream, Dubai South (previously Dubai World Central), which brought all these visions together by linking our airlines and our maritime capabilities. This will be a complete logistics hub that, once completed, will accommodate one million people. The new 'city' will contain Al Maktoum International Airport, which will be the largest in the world serving 160 million travellers every year. This new city will also be connected to Jebel Ali, where today more than 7,000 companies are based, and whose commercial transactions total more than $87 billion every year. We have also built a huge high-speed logistics pathway between the port and the airport so that sea freight can be transferred to air cargo within a few hours.

Our airports connect us to about 200 cities worldwide, and Jebel Ali alone links us with more than 140 cities globally. On top of this are the 78 ports that we manage, which in turn link us to their parent cities. Is Dubai destined to be connected to the world, by merging its airlines and its maritime lines? Is it our fate to become the main airport and seaport of the world? Whenever I remember these incidents that spanned half a century, it is easy to link them all together. Yes, by looking back we can connect the dots, says Jobs. I say, "By looking forward, you can turn dots on paper into realities!"

39

Beirut

The Arab Deterrent Force enters Beirut in an attempt to stop the civil war

Beirut, queen of the world!

      Who sold your bracelets inlaid with sapphires?

Who seized your magic ring and cut your golden nails?

      Who sacrificed the joy in your emerald eyes?

Who slashed your face with a knife

      and burned your lovely lips with acid?

Who poisoned the waters of your sea

      and strewed hatred along your rose shores?

These words, by Nizar Qabbani, reflect what we all feel for the precious city of Beirut, and beautiful Lebanon. My first memories of Beirut date back to the early 1960s when I came from the deserts of Dubai, with its mud houses, sandy streets and palm-covered markets. I travelled to Beirut with my family, passing through on our way to London.

The elegant streets, beautiful neighbourhoods and modern markets of 'the Paris of the Middle East' were an inspiration to me. The energy of its people, the kindness in the way they spoke and how easy it was to get along with them, captivated me. I dreamed that Dubai would one day become like Beirut.

Beirut amazed me as a child and I fell in love with it as a young man. But it would break my heart as an adult.

Whoever visits Beirut will never forget it, and whoever deals with its people, can only return.

A waking dream though it was, Lebanon was fractured and divided into sectarian splinters. It was no longer the Beirut we once knew. Nor was Lebanon itself any longer recognisable.

As Qabbani laments:

> Where is the Beirut who promenades,
>> crowned with blue like a queen?
> Where is the Beirut of our memories?
>> Glittering like a fish in the Mediterranean?
> They killed her
>> They killed her
> She welcomed dawn like jasmine flowers
>> Who gains from the killing of a city?
> My lady, they have lost Beirut.
>> They lost themselves when they lost her.
> She fell like a magic ring in the water,
>> and they did not catch her.
> They chased her like a spring bird,
>> until they killed her.

Over the years, I have often visited Beirut and have many very close friends there. But as Minister of Defence of the United Arab Emirates, I also witnessed two disastrous turning points.

The first was on April 13th, 1975, when the first gunshot went off to announce the start of a civil war that was to last for 15 merciless years, killing more than 150,000 people, maiming around twice that number and causing colossal economic damage, estimated at more than $25 billion. Only a few months after the war broke out, the sound of AK-47s, heavy machine guns and rocket launchers echoed in every part of Beirut as civilian targets were fired upon repeatedly. Piece by piece, the city was being smashed and splintered into sectarian strongholds. That was the beginning of the end.

The elegant streets, beautiful
neighbourhoods and modern
markets were an inspiration to
me. I dreamed that Dubai would
one day become like Beirut

Sheikh Zayed made many efforts to bring the parties and factions together in reconciliation but all his noble attempts failed. I used to help my father during the negotiations, but we were beginning to feel disheartened as we faced one failure after another. Then, a comprehensive Arab intervention was started to prevent further destruction of this beautiful country.

In June 1976 came the second development with the intervention of Syria. I watched quietly the Arab Summit that was taking place in Riyadh, then the Summit in Cairo in October 1976, calling for a ceasefire and the end of the war all over Lebanon. Despite the decisions and the commitments issued during these two summits, I knew that the proposed solutions were only temporary, and that the root causes of the problems were still lingering under the surface. The strongholds of the Lebanese National Movement caused extensive losses to the Syrian forces, but eventually Lebanon became a Syrian province under the rule of the al-Assads.

As an outcome of the Riyadh and Cairo summits, the Arab League formed the Arab Deterrent Force – including troops from the UAE – to enact a truce, stop the bloodshed and establish peace in the country.

In those days, I felt a heavy burden weighing on my shoulders. I did everything I could to prepare my men for their time in Lebanon. I memorised each of their faces and made sure I knew everything about their families, their hopes and their dreams. I understood that I was sending them into danger, a hideous burden for any leader to bear. At the same time, I knew I had to motivate them and rally their spirits. I would say to them, "We are going for the sake of peace, not for the sake of war. We are going to save the nation of our friends and brothers, and not to serve the interests of any group or sect."

By the end of 1976, we had sent 30,000 men from our joint forces and with eyes on the ground I was able to see all angles of the situation. I cannot fully express my loathing for the atrocities of war, and from my personal experiences in combat, I know that it is never the solution.

During the Lebanese Civil War, tens of thousands were killed, and the hundreds of thousands of maimed and injured people remain to remind us of the sadness, fear and hatred that will be passed on to succeeding generations. What a terrible loss to the Arab world that one of its most beautiful cities fell victim to a civil war lasting more than 15 years.

The second encounter involving my beloved Beirut occurred in 1982 and it was even more horrific than the first. In June 1982, the Israeli army under the leadership of Prime Minister Menachem Begin and then Minister of Defence Ariel Sharon invaded Lebanon, which had become a haven for the Palestinian Liberation Organization (PLO), protected by Syria and Iran. Despite the fact that the Israeli invasion was widely expected, no one had anticipated the incomprehensible levels of atrocity it exhibited nor the legacy of bitterness that the operation would leave in its wake.

After two months of sporadic resistance and fighting, a ceasefire agreement was reached. The PLO withdrew from Beirut and headed to Tunis. Under the supervision of the Multinational Force in Lebanon (MNF), Palestinian leaders obtained guarantees regarding the safety of

In a military transport plane delivering relief to the Lebanese people in 1978

civilians in refugee camps. The evacuation of PLO members through the port of Tripoli lasted for two weeks; the Palestinian leader, the late Yasser Arafat, was the last to leave, escorted to the port by a French force. A few days later, on September 9th, 1982, the MNF left Beirut. The next day, Sharon announced that there were still 2,000 'terrorists' living in the Palestinian refugee camps in Beirut. On September 15th, only one day after the departure of the Palestinian fighters, the Israeli army occupied the western part of Beirut, taking full control of Sabra and Shatila, two refugee camps inhabited by Lebanese and Palestinian civilians.

The massacre that followed in Sabra and Shatila was a horrific catastrophe that lasted for 40 hours between September 16th and 18th, 1982. Phalangist militias under the protection of the Israeli army killed, raped and tortured a large number of innocent civilians, mainly women, children and the elderly.

I have never accepted the idea of bloodshed and the meaningless loss of life and can never understand why this continues to happen in our world. I was in touch with all the parties in the region and knew a massacre was about to ensue. When pictures of the victims began to surface on the news, especially those of the women and children, I realised that all our efforts had been in vain. The United Arab Emirates launched an initiative to mitigate the suffering of the Lebanese people. I ordered several C130 aircraft packed with tonnes of humanitarian aid supplies, in one of the biggest operations of its kind in the Gulf. I went with one consignment to visit the camps myself. To this day, the images remain seared into my memory, scarring my heart.

The wounds are always deepest when you have good memories of a place

The wounds are always deepest when you have good memories of a place; when your mind compares the beautiful city of Beirut before and after the war, when your heart compares the kindness and joy of the people of Beirut as it was before, with the scenes of atrocities and killings unfolding in that beautiful city. Unfortunately, Lebanon is still a pawn that many try to manipulate. The youth of Lebanon are still paying the price of unrest in the region, and the country is still an arena of choice for endless conflict – increasingly now involving Iranian-backed Hezbollah forces.

When Lebanon is once again a united home and independent, then it shall again become a welcoming place and inspiration for people from all of the Arab World.

> Oh... Beirut,
> Lady of the golden heart
> Forgive us...
> We made you to fuel and firewood
> For the conflict that tears from the flesh of Arabs

40

The Invasion of a Brother Nation

UAE Armed Forces during their participation in the liberation of Kuwait in 1991

The Iraqi invasion of Kuwait came as one of the biggest shocks of my military life and was seen as an outrage, not just in Dubai and the UAE but across the whole Gulf region.

For us as Emiratis, Kuwait was not just a neighbour. It was truly a part of our lives; our children studied in Kuwaiti schools, our citizens were treated in Kuwaiti clinics and our communities had developed strong economic and social ties to their Kuwaiti brothers and sisters.

The depths of those links is illustrated by one of Dubai's largest and most popular markets, Souq Murshid, named after the Kuwaiti businessman, Fadel Murshid Al Asimi. Furthermore, the development of Dubai's formal education system relied on teachers from Kuwait. My father's biggest project, the expansion of Dubai Creek in the mid 1950s, was partly funded with a loan from Kuwait, while our first television programmes came from Kuwaiti TV, which began broadcasting to Dubai in 1969. The Kuwaiti Hospital, constructed in 1966, was one of the biggest hospitals to serve our people, and remains so to this day. The list is long, the debts owed are many, and the brotherhood between us and between the people of Kuwait is deeper and more profound than many can comprehend. These are connections not to be taken lightly.

The first news of the invasion came early in the morning of August 2nd, 1990. I remember that I asked three times for the officer on the other end of the phone line to repeat what he had just said. I relayed the news to my elder brother Sheikh Maktoum, who was then Crown Prince of Dubai, and I announced a state of emergency for all our military and security forces. I spoke to Sheikh Zayed and found him angry and sad at the same time.

How could Saddam do something like that? And what would come next? We had not expected Saddam to dare invade a brotherly and neighbouring sovereign country, which had always supported him. Saddam's decision to invade Kuwait came as a shock to everyone, and was a major turning point that would transform the whole region.

Suddenly the Gulf became the focus of international news headlines, particularly as it appeared Iraqi armoured forces were poised to sweep southward from Kuwait into Saudi Arabia. A wave of panic broke out and many international companies considered withdrawing from the region. There was an impending run on the banks with international investors looking to relocate funds out of the Gulf as soon as possible. Managers from Dubai International Airport called me to ask for my directions regarding the significant outflow of cash from the country and whether they should restrict it.

UAE Armed Forces during their participation in the liberation of Kuwait in 1991

For us as Emiratis, Kuwait was not just a neighbour. It was truly a part of our lives

My answer to them was: "I do not want you to prevent anyone at the airport from leaving with their money, they can go if they want." I asked them to relay this message to all customs officers. They protested, saying that this might mean our banks would collapse. I replied: "These are my instructions to you. Do not prevent anyone from leaving with their money." A few weeks later, we saw the same people return to Dubai with their money. Had we tried to stop them, we would have increased their concerns and made them think that our banks were unable to pay out. We were able to prove that, despite looming threats, things did not change in Dubai.

We received tens of thousands of our Kuwaiti brothers and sisters. We welcomed them in our hotels and residential buildings and many of our people opened their homes, and their hearts, to them. Our ports became berths for the US Navy and British Royal Navy as a coalition assembled to protect the region under Operation Desert Shield, evolving into Operation Desert Storm for the liberation of Kuwait, launched on January 16th, 1991. We opened up military

The invasion of Kuwait
ended with the Iraqi forces
withdrawing in disgrace.
That was not the end of the
story, but the beginning of a
new era in the region

airports and cleared ports and warehouses to make way for the build-up of coalition forces. Jebel Ali Port received more coalition ships than any other port, because it was the largest and the best equipped in the Gulf.

Our military forces made a direct contribution to the coalition offensive to free Kuwait, and I personally travelled to the headquarters of the Desert Storm operation several times. My priority, when dealing with General Norman Schwarzkopf, the Commander of the International Coalition Forces, who was leading more than 900,000 soldiers, was to find ways to minimise civilian casualties and collateral damage. It was clear that neither the peoples of Kuwait nor Iraq had wanted this invasion. It was Saddam's foolish move and I was adamant in trying to protect the Iraqi people from having to pay the price for his recklessness.

UAE Armed Forces during their participation in the liberation of Kuwait in 1991

Eventually, in February 1992, Saddam was forced to withdraw after a successful military operation and Emirati forces had the honour of being the first to enter Kuwait in order to liberate the country. We are indebted to Kuwait and, had the occasion arisen, we would have given our lives to free it. One of my proudest memories of that difficult time was the huge surge of young people volunteering to join our armed forces. The enthusiasm of the people in the recruitment centres was amazing, bringing us much joy. It was a true expression of the sincere, heartfelt patriotism that countries need in order to overcome times of war, and to build and flourish in times of peace.

The invasion of Kuwait ended with the Iraqi forces withdrawing in disgrace. That was not the end of the story, but the beginning of a new era in the region, an era which commenced with the fall of a great nation and the dissolution of a powerful army. The invasion of Kuwait was a mistake of epic proportions, with far-reaching consequences that changed the face of the Middle East forever.

41

There Are No
Winners in War

Sheikh Zayed bin Sultan with Saddam Hussein in 1982

I still remember when the devastating war between Iraq and Iran ended, leaving more than a million people dead in its wake. War never ends as swiftly as it erupts; instead its damage lasts for years, even decades. That is how it was with Iraq.

Once, when Iraqi president Saddam Hussein was at the peak of his self-proclaimed glory and grandiosity, I remember that he expressed his reservations about me to Sheikh Zayed saying, "He is inclined towards the West and does not treat Arabs well." As a result, Sheikh Zayed, as was his nature, God rest his soul, asked me to meet with Saddam to resolve any matters that could affect our interests.

I met Saddam first on the sidelines of a regional meeting. Our talk began with the normal pleasantries and platitudes before Saddam got to what was really on his mind. He told me he had a report saying that we had been supporting Iran, and he set it in front of me. I answered, "I do not need a report. I am here with you. If you mean shipments of arms, I challenge anyone to show that is true. But if you mean shipments of food, then yes. And we do not need any reports to tell us that because our ships do go there and to Iraq as well. I would never stop any humanitarian aid from reaching people."

He appeared surprised at the boldness of my response. He was used to being told what he wanted to hear. And perhaps my reply came as a surprise because he hadn't expected me to push back at him. But following that first encounter, we became friends.

With the invasion of Kuwait, all bridges were broken. But in the world of politics, it is important to keep a small line of communication open for times of crisis.

> **"**
> Our talk began with the
> normal pleasantries and
> platitudes before Saddam got
> to what was really on his mind.
> 'I have a report saying that you
> have been supporting Iran'
> **"**

After the liberation of Kuwait in February 1991, the entire Gulf region was hurt, winner and loser alike. All were trying to bury their pain and rebuild what had been destroyed. Iraq was weary of wars and yet still Saddam Hussein, the defeated leader, could not sleep easy.

In 2003, the Americans returned to the Middle East. They wanted to build a region based on their own concepts, especially after September 11th, 2001, an event that changed how they saw our region and rearranged their priorities. I knew that war with Iraq was a goal for George W. Bush. We tried to convince him not to invade. I asked him to invest his money and energy into helping the people of Iraq rebuild their schools and hospitals and pave their streets instead, but I realised he was resolute in his decision to use force. I requested the Americans give us a chance to intervene. I asked, "What do you want from Saddam?"

I knew that the consequences of a war, on the region in general and on Iraq in particular, would be disastrous. I tried to convince the Americans to allow our leaders to negotiate. After all, we are Arabs, sharing similar traditions and traits, and we understand how Saddam and his kind actually think.

I decided to visit Saddam in person. I took a flight from Dubai to Bahrain, and from there travelled by sea towards Basra. We met in one of his hideouts and we began an honest and direct conversation. We spoke about everything: areas on which we agreed and those, rather more numerous, on which we disagreed. I reminded him of the lingering repercussions of war, knowing very well that I was advising a man who had spent a good deal of his life in conflict. It was obvious that he could not win against the United States and if he did not do something to prevent the impending attack, Iraq would lose everything. I tried to use logic and reason with him. I said softly, "If you are forced to leave the presidency in order to protect Iraq, then do it. Dubai is your second home and you are always welcome there."

He looked at me and said, "Sheikh Mohammed, I am talking about protecting Iraq, not myself." I could only respect that basic attitude – though I profoundly disagreed with his concept of 'protection'.

Our meeting, which was honest but tense, lasted for about five hours, during which Saddam got up and left four times, breeching protocol. Every time he came back, he would ask for some Arabic coffee before we continued our talk. I still recall the taste of it. He terrified everyone who attended the meeting with us, including Abed Hamoud, his private secretary. Every time he left, I would pray to God that we

> **"**
>
> Following the invasion, Iraq was not the same and neither was the region. I warned the Americans about engaging in warfare in the region, saying, 'Do not open Pandora's Box'
>
> **"**

would get through this latest hiatus. Saddam would not sit in the same place for long. He was afraid of being shot; he knew that he was a target for many potential assassins.

When the meeting ended, he escorted me to the car, opened the door for me, and said goodbye – something that I was told he did not usually do. I travelled to Amman and from there took a flight back to my homeland.

During the Arab Summit held in Sharm El Sheikh in March 2003, days before the Iraq invasion, Sheikh Zayed proposed to Saddam that he seek asylum in Abu Dhabi, as a last attempt to try to avoid the impending blitz. It was too late in the day and the United States had already made the decision to launch Operation Iraqi Freedom. The United States and the United Kingdom came in with their powerful tanks, artillery and air power, and once again Iraq began to bleed. Saddam had grossly miscalculated. He thought that instilling terror and panic, using the sword, was the right way to manage things. And because everyone around him lived in fear, they were not brave enough to be honest about the true capabilities of his forces. They preferred to make him believe that he had the ability to fight the Americans. No one can rule with the power of fear for long, and Saddam paid a heavy price for this. His people paid a much heavier price, time and again.

We did not believe that he owned weapons of mass destruction (WMDs), as London and Washington claimed. Even General Colin Powell, who was US Secretary of State at the time, later expressed his regret for the destruction that the Americans inflicted during the Iraq invasion. He was to admit that the weapons inspectors did not find any trace of the alleged WMDs and that the justification for the war on Iraq was flawed and a blot on his political career.

Following the invasion, Iraq was not the same and neither was the region. I warned the Americans about engaging in warfare in the region, saying, "Do not open Pandora's Box. There are many surprises in it."

Iraq lost many souls and decades of development. The Americans and British lost more than a trillion dollars, around 5,000 dead and some 35,000 wounded. Iraqi casualties were a hundred times that, along with a whole decade of lost development and terrible schisms in its society. From Iraq there emerged groups who went on to terrorise the entire world. Just as history has taught us time and again, there are no winners in war.

42

Bashar al-Assad's Syria

With Bashar al-Assad and Omar Sharif in Palmyra, Syria, in 1999

Water begins in Damascus; for wherever
you lay your head there is a spring.
Time begins in Damascus, and in it
languages endure and lineages continue.

Since my youth and throughout adulthood, Syria to me has been one of the most important nations in the region. The home of civilisation, quintessentially Arab, Syria was the land of nature and beauty, history and culture.

They say that civilisation in Syria dates back at least eight millennia, that it has been home to 40 civilisations and that human civilisation began in Syria, with the rise of the alphabet and of agriculture.

Syria sparks many emotions in the heart of every Arab, be it feelings of love for its people and its civilisation, or of sadness for the war and destruction that have gripped it.

As I reminisce about beloved Syria, I recall the late 1990s when Bashar al-Assad visited Dubai. At that time his father, Hafez al-Assad, was the president. It was possibly his last days as such and the question of Bashar al-Assad taking power was only a matter of time. I wanted Bashar al-Assad to spend some private time with me, away from his entourage. Among them was a friend of his called Manaf Tlas, son of the Syrian Minister of Defence at the time, Mustafa Tlas.

I asked an official to go with the escorting delegation in one car and asked Bashar al-Assad to accompany me. I drove, as usual. The convoy followed and at some point, as we entered the city, I gave orders to the convoy to make a right turn, while I turned left without any warning.

In the car mirror I saw that the convoy had followed my order as requested, and soon I saw the cars all come to a halt. His security men emerged and started sprinting towards us because they could not turn their cars around in the traffic. My car, however, soon slipped away and we were out of view. It was just like a scene from a movie! Sitting in the passenger seat, al-Assad asked me what was going on. I said to him, "I thought it would be a nice idea to experience Dubai away from all the formality and protocol."

With Bashar al-Assad in Dubai in 1999

> Syria sparks many
> emotions in the heart of
> every Arab, be it feelings of
> love for its people and its
> civilisation, or of sadness
> for the war and destruction
> that have gripped it

We proceeded to a large mall, a popular destination for shoppers from around the world. We got out of the car and started walking around and talking together. No one bothered us and we spoke about the future of technology and its role in developing nations. He was head of the Syrian Computer Society and he was enthusiastic about investing in technology to enhance the development of Syria and its people. He also seemed to enjoy our car ride adventure. We had a good relationship from that day onwards.

A few years later, he visited Dubai again, but this time he came as President Bashar al-Assad. He asked me, "How does the government of Dubai manage its city?" He had a genuine desire to develop Syria's government and administration.

> I sincerely hope that Syria will one day succeed in healing and resurrecting its broken society. The Syrian people, who built 40 civilisations, are capable of building a better new one

I spoke to him at length about Dubai, its openness and its adoption of a private sector mindset in the management of government, in terms of providing outstanding services, spending money in a highly efficient manner, building the capacity of its personnel and developing skilled leaders. I told him that we hoped to build a model for the Arab world, but that we ourselves were learning and benefitting from both Arab and international experiences.

I remember taking him to the Dubai School of Government, now known as Mohammed bin Rashid School of Government, a college we built to train our staff in line with the best management systems in the field, and in cooperation with other institutions. On occasion, we also host groups of government officials from Arab countries who come to receive training in advanced methods of government administration.

President al-Assad was very impressed. At the end of his visit he expressed his admiration for the Dubai model, insisting that he would recreate it in Syria.

At the beginning of his reign, al-Assad tried to liberalise the economy in Syria: allowing foreign banks to open, enabling citizens to open foreign currency accounts and inviting foreign investors to invest in Syria. I remember that I sent a delegation there to identify potential investment opportunities and they came back to me with some good ideas.

He was then dragged into a very different world, watching the bloodshed and destruction that rained down on Syria, devouring anything in its way and despoiling a civilised culture that dates back millennia.

I read a United Nations report about the ravages of the Syrian war; more than 400,000 dead – most of them civilians – five million refugees forced to leave the country, six million internally displaced persons and about $400 billion in infrastructural damages.

I sincerely hope that Syria will one day succeed in healing and resurrecting its broken society. The Syrian people, who built 40 civilisations, are capable of building a better new one. Of this, I am utterly convinced.

43

The Departure
of Rashid

They asked me why I did not lament my father,

     when lamenting a father is a debt we owe.

You who blame, how unjust you are,

     when I have no mind left to express how I feel.

With Sheikh Zayed at the funeral of my father Sheikh Rashid in 1990

One of the hardest moments is having to say goodbye to someone you love, goodbye to the person who was responsible for your existence, the reason for your life, the reason for your success, and the reason for the presence of your country in which you live in bliss.

The last formal occasion when Sheikh Rashid appeared in public was during the reception he held in honour of the Indian Prime Minister at the time, Indira Ghandi. That was in May of 1981. After that, the signs of fatigue began to appear. All those who knew Sheikh Rashid knew him to be a physically strong man, alert, never tiring and never succumbing to exhaustion. He only slept for one hour at most in the afternoon, and about five hours at night.

His life revolved around his work and he was always on the move; negotiating, discussing and following up on issues. He was well versed in politics, economics, finance and business. He was a wise man, a visionary architect. In his *majlis*, he welcomed people from near and far, locals and visitors, rich and poor.

He liked to listen more than he liked to talk, and he was extremely down to earth, to such an extent that it was hard for those who did not know him to believe he was the ruler. I remember in 1966, oil company engineers came to his office at the customs department, requesting to see the ruler to impart good news regarding a new oil find. They found a man sitting at a small wooden desk covered with many scattered papers and files. They sat and spoke to him about this great discovery and explained to him how important it was. Then they asked him when Sheikh Rashid, the ruler, was coming so that they could meet with him and tell him personally. He said to them, "I am Rashid."

One of the hardest moments is having to say goodbye to someone you love

At the beginning, they did not believe him, until he reassured them, joining in their laughter when they realised he was telling the truth.

In May of 1981 Sheikh Rashid become increasingly ill and visibly tired. I suggested he move to a resthouse in the mountains in Hatta in order to renew his energy and enjoy some respite and solitude for a while. He liked the idea, but he soon found he missed the bustle and energy of Dubai, the constant movement that he had created through his endless projects. So he returned to the city. On the way back, his health suddenly took a turn for the worse and we moved him to his palace in Zabeel. The news that Sheikh Rashid was ill spread very quickly among the population and we received many friendly and supportive messages. The people began to worry about the father, and architect, of modern Dubai, the man who, along with Sheikh Zayed, created this nation in which previous hardships had been replaced by prosperity. Within days, Sheikh Rashid regained his strength and he began to receive calls from his brother Sheikh Zayed and the other rulers of the emirates wishing him well. I suggested he travel to London to undergo tests and receive treatment. On June 20th, 1981, he arrived in London. A few hours after he arrived, he

The funeral prayer for the soul of the late Sheikh Rashid bin Saeed in 1990

received the then Prime Minister, Margaret Thatcher, who came to inquire about his health. Her Majesty Queen Elizabeth II also called several times to check on his progress. Sheikh Rashid surprised his physicians with his speedy recovery. He was anxious to come back to Dubai, and was ready to work harder and give more.

My father's recovery was to prove short-lived. The death of my mother, in 1983, dealt him an awful blow. Sadness became his constant companion; a permanent downcast expression in his eyes only noticeable to those who knew he had lost his closest friend of more than 40 years. The death of Sheikha Latifa was a major setback to his health, for it was as if two souls had been cleaved from each other. With her death, she took part of him, but she also left behind many parts of herself. My sisters would spend all day by his bedside until 3pm, when he would receive close friends. In 1990, he reached the age of 78. And despite the signs of weakness that were beginning to show, he was alert, a sharp thinker. He spoke wisely and had depth of vision. What made him happiest during the final days of his life was sitting by the window in his palace in Zabeel, looking out over Dubai. He could see the city that he had designed and built emerging, after sacrificing his days and nights for its sake.

At 10am on Sunday, October 7th, 1990, Rashid's soul returned to its maker and he left this world gently and peacefully. Hearts mourned his death, tears were shed. Many did not believe that Rashid, who had been a father to them for over three decades, was dead. The death of a father is perhaps the most difficult death to accept.

With my brothers Sheikh Maktoum and Sheikh Hamdan at the condolences meeting for our father Sheikh Rashid bin Saeed in 1990

On the Monday, the funeral procession of Sheikh Rashid, may God bless his soul, set out on his final journey. My brother Sheikh Hamdan drove the vehicle carrying his coffin, while Sheikh Zayed rode in the second car in a convoy of vehicles bearing heavy, grieving hearts.

When we arrived at the cemetery, Sheikh Hamdan and I helped to carry his body to his final resting place, through the thousands of people from Dubai and the other emirates who attended his funeral. They shed tears for him, remembering all of his achievements and goodness. Among the thousands mourning Sheikh Rashid were many Europeans, Asians, Africans and Americans who had come to Dubai and helped build the city, attracted by Sheikh Rashid's international vision. They, too, were part of his huge legacy, creating a truly global and cosmopolitan city, free from any form of discrimination based on gender, ethnicity, colour or religion, all at peace under one umbrella. While living here, they could feel safe personally, secure financially and confident to build a future for themselves and for their children.

In New York, the United Nations General Assembly stood in silence for a minute in mourning for Sheikh Rashid, and the news of his death was widely broadcast, along with all of his achievements – principally in creating the economic and developmental miracle that is Dubai. When I saw the tears in the eyes of the humble labourers, I realised that Sheikh Rashid had touched the hearts of everyone, and that his morning walks and tours were not limited to visiting projects, but were also to visit the public. His mark is found on every stone, in every corner of Dubai, whose construction he personally supervised, so that his legacy shall remain forever alive in the memory of his nation and his people.

44

A New Dubai
in Africa

With Muammar Gaddafi in 2010

Many leaders who have visited Dubai have said how they wished their countries could be like this unique city. Many have contacted me and I have met with leaders wishing to replicate the Dubai experience in their own countries. For most of them, however, this has been just a dream because they have been unable to see behind the amazing buildings and infrastructure to understand the ideas and realities on which they are based.

There is a big difference between wishing for something and working to realise those dreams. The gap between wishes and reality needs to be filled with determination and perseverance. It needs to be filled with plans, money and men. It's a vast gap that requires endless work.

My days in Dubai begin at 6am. I know all of my projects. I monitor all of my plans. With our projects, we build human capacity and leaders to advance them, ensure their continuity and achieve world-class standards. Every day, I delegate authority to young men and women, striving to empower them to lead their country and add their contribution to it. We do not tolerate corruption, we do not undermine the rule of the law, nor are we lax in the implementation of the plans we launch. That is how we are building Dubai today.

Our experience is open to any nation or government that wishes to duplicate it in its entirety. I am often asked if I am afraid of competition. My reply is always, "If our Arab world had ten cities like Dubai, we would be blessed." If Dubai was part of a thriving, prosperous region, its own development would accelerate exponentially. Dubai needs strong sister cities to work with, hand-in-hand, to create new miracles of global proportions. That is how we view competition. If the economy in the region were to improve, personal income were to increase and the number of educated, talented individuals were to rise, then Dubai would be ten times better off. A rising tide raises all boats.

As I write this, I am reminded of the late Libyan leader, Muammar Gaddafi, who called me one day saying he wanted to build a new Dubai-style city in Libya to serve as Africa's economic capital. After the Americans invaded Iraq in 2003, searching for weapons of mass destruction that they claimed Saddam Hussein possessed, Gaddafi announced to the world that Libya would give up its nuclear weapons programme. He reached out to other leaders, seeking the removal of any materials and equipment that could lead to the development of nuclear weapons and weapons of mass destruction, opening up a future of scientific prosperity and technological development. I was one of those leaders and what Gaddafi was asking for was my assistance in building a new Dubai in Libya, underscoring his professed desire to open up to the world. I sent Mohammad Al Gergawi, the head of my Executive Office at the time, to carry a message to Libya. Two days after his arrival, Gaddafi's men escorted him to the Bab Al Azizia in Tripoli. He waited to be shown into a large room, where he found Gaddafi sitting at his desk browsing the internet in a way that aimed to demonstrate his technical savvy but succeeded only in betraying his awkwardness with computers. Gaddafi started by saying, "I admire what Sheikh Mohammed has done in Dubai and I want to do the same in Libya. I would like you to invest in Libya and I would also like your expertise in making this new dream come true for the Libyan people."

He specifically asked that we look at transforming Tripoli and the airport of Mitiga to make a new capital for Africa. They talked together, during which time my envoy formed the impression that Gaddafi had little knowledge of history or current affairs and that the team around him kept him in the dark, either on purpose or, I strongly suspect, out of fear. It was a long and meaningless conversation. My envoy summed it up saying, "Gaddafi admires no nation, nor any leader. He expresses his opinions with a fanaticism that makes it hard to have any type of discussion. He does not talk like a leader." After reading Mohammad Al Gergawi's report, I decided to go myself. I flew to Tripoli, a beautiful city with a rich, vibrant history. Whenever I visit a city, I prefer to tour it on my own or with a very small team, to discover it better without the escorts and protocol that prevent you from seeing the reality of a place.

On the first day, we visited the old town, a desolate location that made me feel sad. How could a country that had so much wealth descend to this? Sewage in the streets, garbage strewn all over. Even Dubai back in the 1950s, when resources were limited, water was scarce and electricity almost non-existent, was not as depressing.

Later I visited Gaddafi in his tent in the city of Sirte and, just like the last time we had met, he monopolised the entire conversation. In the evening, we went to one of Tripoli's public squares, which was packed with people. We were surprised to find that someone had told the people we were there. They surrounded the car in a hysterical frenzy, with emotions running high, and the car began to rock because of the jostling and pushing. Moments later, I began to feel that our car was being lifted off the ground. I found such exuberance troublesome, even if it was meant to be welcoming and a true expression of emotion. I wasn't able to make myself heard over their shouting.

The guards then took over and dispersed the crowd quite violently. This, too, disturbed me. I never wanted them to be sent away like that.

Gaddafi wanted to show me the Green Mountain region, north-east of Tripoli, where there are Greek and Roman ruins. We boarded an aeroplane with Saif Al Islam Gaddafi, the leader's son, and Abdullah Al Sanoussi, head of internal security and military intelligence at the time, who was also related to Gaddafi and was notorious for being a violent, grim-faced man. The plane took off and once it reached cruising altitude, Sanoussi turned to me and said, "This is the first time I have been on an aeroplane for a while." When I asked why, he answered, "I have always been a target and I am afraid they might target the aircraft I am in."

I sat there mulling over his words in silence. Had he wanted his first time back on a plane to be with me?

Saif Al Islam spoke and it sounded like he was more knowledgeable than his father. He said, "I have always been curious about the economy that my father adopted, for it is neither socialist nor communist, nor even capitalist." He added, "I have often spoken to him about the importance of the land being returned to the people and of us being more open to the world."

After the visit ended, I found that the people of Libya lingered in my heart. I had hoped to help them, but things did not go well. I withdrew from the talks about the new project after I realised that we were running around in circles, that the whole issue was shrouded in clouds of corruption and that we were setting ourselves up to be used merely as collateral in Gaddafi's propaganda schemes. Gaddafi wished for the appearance of change but did not want true transformation. Change needs real achievements and hard work, not simply empty speeches. Change cannot happen with the scale of corruption we witnessed during our visits to Libya. Change needs a clear, clean and transparent environment to flourish.

The Libyan people did not need Mohammed bin Rashid to show them how to create a better society – they were quite capable of turning things around for themselves. As we found in the UAE, the government's job is merely to create an enabling environment: the people will do the rest. The Libyan nation was full of scientists, talented individuals, executives, researchers, physicians and engineers; all they needed was the right environment to unleash their potential and bring about positive change.

I gave an example to a leader once during a conference on the role of governments. I asked him about the job of a traffic policeman standing in the middle of a busy intersection. He said the policeman was there to direct the traffic coming from all directions and make sure no accidents occurred. So I asked him what would happen if he prevented everyone from moving, except his friends and relatives. He answered, "He would be a failure, a corrupt person who is not performing his duties."

Governments are the traffic police and their role is to facilitate the movement of life for the people who are driven to build their futures and their nations. Unfortunately, our region suffers from an excess of failed traffic policemen.

45

The Departure of Zayed

The funeral of Sheikh Zayed bin Sultan

There are two kinds of people: those who live life and those who give life. Zayed bin Sultan was among the latter. He added to the life of his nation, benefitting millions of people through his wisdom and insight. That is true immortality. Sheikh Zayed taught us that a person can remain alive in the hearts and minds of humanity. He taught us that a person can remain elevated in life, even after death.

I often accompanied Sheikh Zayed, and I learned so much from him. I learned to look for areas of agreement instead of discord, to look towards the future instead of the past, to look for factors that unite us, make us stronger and elevate us. That was how Sheikh Zayed worked to unite the United Arab Emirates, and had it not been for his wisdom, the country would not be where it is today. Sheikh Zayed was the founder of the United Arab Emirates, its first President, the first to draft laws and legislation and the first to lay the cornerstone for the country's development. Sheikh Zayed was the first in everything, and the first always holds a special place in people's hearts.

Sheikh Zayed became the Ruler of Al Ain in 1946 when he was only 28 years old. The tribes loved him and his men rallied around him as he began his great journey in the middle of the desert. He dug wells with his own hands alongside the *Bedu*, helped build the *aflaj* (irrigation channels), and did not let the lack of water and funds stand in his way. He built the first school, the first marketplace, the first clinic and the first modern road network. He will always be the first. The people loved him because he would sit on the ground and eat with them, talk to them and consult them. He would work beside them as an equal. From the simplicity of Al Ain, Sheikh Zayed continued his journey without conceit or a sense of personal grandeur, succeeding in ruling with wisdom for the half century that he gave to his nation.

I learned so much from Zayed.
I learned to look for areas of
agreement instead of discord,
to look towards the future
instead of the past

In 1953, 13 years before becoming the Ruler of Abu Dhabi, Sheikh Zayed went on a tour that included the United States, United Kingdom, France, Switzerland, Egypt, Iraq and India, among other countries. He came back from this trip full of conviction, dreams and determination; conviction that his people deserved to live like the people in those nations, dreams of building a state similar to those countries and determination never to give up on his dream until his last breath.

Sheikh Zayed, may he rest in peace, began working towards his dream, never stopping nor tiring until his death in 2004. His achievements will remain alive all around us so long as this nation exists. I accompanied Sheikh Zayed to many events and meetings, as well as in times of crisis. If I were to describe him using only one word, I would say 'wise'. Wisdom is a great treasure that God Almighty chooses to bestow on certain people; "and whoever has been given wisdom has certainly been given much good". (The Quran, 2:269).

The founding leaders of the GCC in Abu Dhabi in 1981

He was wise in the way he dealt with the oil money that flowed into his government. There are many oil-rich countries in the world, but very few possess the wisdom of Sheikh Zayed. He used that income to create sustainable development for his people, to build a nation out of nothing, to empower people who are capable of carrying his dream forward. His financial wisdom was way ahead of its time. He established a sovereign fund that would safeguard most of the money and invest it for generations to come. He was thinking of his grandchildren and their grandchildren – the future generations of Emiratis. That sovereign fund is now one of the largest in the world.

Sheikh Zayed was also wise when it came to managing the Union. He won the hearts of the rulers of the other six emirates from the start, and the hearts of the people as well. He resolved disputes between neighbours decisively, and dedicated his efforts and energy to development, building and construction projects. His modesty captivated young people, his generosity captivated hearts and his

> He who builds nations does not
> die. He who empowers leaders
> does not die. He who lives a
> good life does not die

projects captivated the imagination. All this was achieved through the wisdom that God bestowed upon Sheikh Zayed.

The people of other Arab nations also loved Sheikh Zayed for his wisdom. He worked hard to establish the Gulf Cooperation Council with Sheikh Jaber Al Sabah, the Emir of Kuwait at that time, hosting its first meeting in Abu Dhabi in May of 1981. He successfully resolved a conflict between the Sultanate of Oman and South Yemen in the 1980s. During that same period, he also called for an Arab League Summit to end the war in Lebanon, and acted as a mediator between Libya and Egypt to resolve their disputes. He was the first to call for Egypt's return to the Arab League following the uproar about its signature of the Camp David peace agreement with Israel. He was the first to call for reconciliation between Iraq and Kuwait after the first Gulf War, and he tried to prevent the American bombardment of Iraq by asking the Iraqi president to leave the country, offering to host him in Abu Dhabi. He also participated in United Nations peacekeeping efforts in war-torn Somalia by sending Emirati troops with the international forces in early 1993. There are many other decisions and instances that bear witness to Sheikh Zayed's determination to reach agreements and extinguish the fires of discord, to unite citizens and eliminate disparity.

People loved Sheikh Zayed because he loved people. He had a boundless love for humanity. Sheikh Zayed gave without expecting anything in return. I personally learned from him how to give privately, for the donations he made privately amounted to much more than those which he gave publicly. He was a man with a big heart and there was always sincerity in his deeds.

This is probably one of the reasons people loved him so much. It seemed that God loved him and placed love for him in people's hearts. It is not surprising that Zayed's memory is like an object of value; the more I recall it, the more it shines, and the more time passes, the more valuable it becomes.

Sheikh Zayed died peacefully on November 2nd, 2004, but Emiratis continue to live with him every day. They live by his unforgettable legacy. They live by his wisdom, which the people remember and use as a compass to continue his journey.

Even after his death, we cherish Sheikh Zayed's great wisdom. He who builds nations does not die. He who empowers leaders does not die. He who lives a good life does not die.

He is, with his Lord, living on in people's hearts forever.
May your final abode be Paradise, beloved Sheikh Zayed.

46

The Finest Horse in the World

With Dubai Millennium after winning a race in Deauville, France, in 1999

A Western friend once asked me while we were having dinner after a horse race in the United Kingdom, "You are one of the most successful racehorse owners in the world, what does owning such magnificent horses mean to you?"

I was puzzled for a few moments by his question, not because I did not know how to answer it, but because the answer could not be summarised in just a few sentences. Horses, for the Arabs, are linked to honour, social status and magnanimity. The connection that Arabs have with horses stretches back more than nine millennia to the time when horses were first domesticated in the Arabian Peninsula. The Arabs discovered that a horse can be one of man's best friends. They found out how intelligent, loyal and patient they were, so they forged close bonds with them. From this bond grew the Arabian horse, known for its loyalty, speed and intelligence.

An Arab treats his horses in the same way he treats his children, caring for them day and night, talking and listening to them. In return, the horse gives him devotion, protection, care, and will not let him down in times of need, conflict or adversity.

Arab history records a war that lasted for 40 years, the Dais and Al Ghabra War between the tribes of the Bani Abs and Dhubyan, which broke out because of cheating during a horse race. I am not proud of that war, for the blood of the people is more precious and honourable, but it is proof of the special status horses hold in the minds and hearts of the Arab people.

My father once told me a story about a horse named Kaheelah. She was owned by a great sheikh, and was like no other horse.

She possessed remarkable grace, speed and stamina. Her speed was, as a poet once described:

> To charge, retreat, and wheel – as strong and fast
> as boulders, flung down from high by floods.

And her beauty was, as another poet said:

> As if God Himself had created it for us to feast our eyes on

Because of her remarkable breed, Kaheelah was the talk of the tribes, and everyone coveted her. However, the sheikh absolutely refused to give her up or to sell her. One of the sheikhs of another tribe tried repeatedly to get his hands on her. He offered blandishments, money and treasure. He even offered an alliance which would strengthen the man's power. Yet Kaheelah's owner refused time and again.

The elder therefore plotted against him, and was adamant to have Kaheelah, even if that meant resorting to theft. The man sent one of his riders, disguised as a poor and needy man to Kaheelah's owner, begging to join his retinue and the noble sheikh accepted him.

The rider began working as a camel herder, a position that allowed him to start gathering information about Kaheelah and get closer to the sheikh's daughter to know more about the coveted horse. He succeeded in discovering that Kaheelah was taken out every afternoon to graze in one of the pastures nearby, and would come back before nightfall with her groom.

The rider kept track of all Kaheelah's movements, the time she left and the time she came back. He had his reins on hand at all times, waiting for the right time to pounce and steal her. It took only a few seconds when the caretaker looked away, for the rider to grab the opportunity, spring on the horse, rein her in and speed off with her.

The news spread like wild fire and reached Kaheelah's stunned owner, the sheikh, and his son. They sped towards the stables, mounted their horses and rode after the thief until they caught up with him. He was a stranger and he did not know the paths of the desert where Kaheelah's owner lived. The sheikh's son was riding a horse called Baleeq, a lowly horse of unknown breed. The thief saw them coming, and without realising what he was doing, he rode into a large area of soft sand. Kaheelah forged ahead with great difficulty, while the lowly horse Baleeq was cantering on solid ground, and was therefore able to close the distance between them.

Horror was reflected clearly on the sheikh's face, and he shouted at the top of his voice to the thief, "Take her to the left, the land there is even. Take her to the left, the land there is solid!" The thief steered her to the smooth ground, and she took off with a speed that made it impossible for anyone to catch up with her. The son stared at his father angrily, and asked him why he had led the thief to even ground. The sheikh answered, "So that it would not be said that a horse of unknown breed caught up with my lovely Kaheelah!"

That is how much the Arabs loved their horses. The sheikh preferred to give her up in order to protect her reputation, name and status among the tribes.

I owned a horse that I loved in the same way that the sheikh loved Kaheelah. As a young horse, he was named Yaazer and he was the finest horse I have ever owned. Our foals carried stable names until we understood their true capabilities and I changed his name when I realised what he was made from.

From the moment I set eyes on Yaazer as a foal, I knew he would be a great horse. It is possible to see the markings of a great horse early on. Just by looking into their eyes, you can tell so much. Look at what the horses see! Some of them are afraid and swish their tails the minute they see a stranger passing in front of them, while some horses do not move and just stare at strange things out of curiosity, and in a challenging manner. The way horses look at things will tell you if the horse is destined to be a leader or a follower.

Wide-set eyes on a horse are like the truthful, smiling face of a human being and are a sign of honesty and loyalty. However, it is not just the size of the eyes, but also their depth and the way they shine, like endless oceans.

Small, mean eyes do not necessarily indicate that the horse is not talented, or lacks capabilities, but they surely suggest that he is not ready or is unwilling to use those capabilities and talents. Laughing eyes, or eyes that speak, indicate the ease with which you can raise and care for that horse. Then there are horses that are capable of looking into the eyes of their opponents, dominating them and flicking their heads when they have summed up their foe. They even challenge their trainers if they miscalculate the exceptional capabilities of the horse.

He had soft, shiny skin,
through which you could see
hundreds of veins, especially the
artery leading from the heart,
which reflected the life and
energy that beat in his veins

The face of a horse also speaks volumes about him. Ears that are far apart are a sign of the greatness of a horse because the structure of the skull is reflected in the location of the ears. What lies between the ears is a rich and wide forehead. This feature is a sign of the size of the horse's brain. However, having such features is not a sign of speed so much as a sign that the horse is able to understand the task at hand and so react well to any situation that requires speed.

As for the openings of the nostrils, they indicate that a horse is a sports horse. When these openings are big and wide, the horse is able to take in a large amount of oxygen. Besides large, wide nostrils mean that the horse has large lungs that are able to store oxygen during breathing.

A wide mouth is also a sign of a horse's strength and speed, which indicates that the trachea is large and that the location where the trachea is found is also large. The jaw must therefore protrude towards the neck in a large space, but the way the neck drops and the way it extends from the body must also be ideal at the right angle.

The most important feature to judge a horse by is probably its gait. Horses possess specific ratios that govern the way they walk. You can tell by a horse's walk how consistent it is to those ideal ratios.

There was one horse, and one horse only that I owned in my life, which had ideal features and measurements. He had beautiful ears that were far apart, with fine tips like the ends of a feather. His forehead was wide, on dainty bones shaped like an inverted pyramid.

The muscles over his eyebrows were also shaped like pyramids, which covered his beautiful, brilliant eyes. As for his nose, it had two wide nostrils that were able to inhale a large quantity of air. His neck was long with pride and vigour. The lower half of his body was huge, double the size of most other horses of his age.

He had soft, shiny skin through which you could see hundreds of veins, especially the artery leading from the heart, which was very distinct, large and wide, as if it reflected the life and energy that beat in his veins. His chest was broad and his back was supported by a strong bone structure, covered in a layer of muscles.

The most beautiful thing about his tail was that it was not high, nor low, it was in the right place, as if it was the perfect ending to his spinal cord. It was impossible not to notice the width of his thighs, or the way he stood or walked.

He had wide eyes that overflowed with grandness and pride, without even a trace of fear in them. He had strong, powerful eyes, which were kind and gentle at the same time. He was large and arrogant, with a dominant bearing. He could intimidate any inexperienced rider. He was like a ball of fire, always full of life and energy.

I would visit him in my stables in the Al Qouz area in Dubai. I would sit there and look at this beautiful creature with awe. He would slide his head under my arm, and put out his tongue so I could give him some carrots, which I always kept hidden on me. Whenever I stroked his neck, he was very happy.

I would sit beside him and we would stare at each other. I would sit on the fodder box, which was about the height of his chest. When he walked beside me, he was the same height as I was. He would lift his hind leg and then relax it, then rest his head in front of me as if he were a bird resting in my presence. It was the ultimate trust displayed by such a strong beast.

What pleasure I used to feel when that great giant of a horse shared these moments with me. I was happy just to sit with him there, and look at him with love and admiration, for hours.

He was the greatest horse that I have ever owned, Dubai Millennium, and his story was remarkable indeed.

47

Dubai Millennium

Dubai Millennium

Who taught the horses to call me by my name
and to greet me from afar?
I come near, they rejoice, playful;
I'm absent, they await me, anxious.
They sense my presence, recognise me,
excited and whinny their greetings
They know my heart, sniff my hands,
as if they are saying they feel as I do.
When I come to them after a long absence, they greet me;
the stables come alive with their cries
as if they are crying out, how lovely to see you again,
how long you have been away!
Horses have breeds, nations and countries.
They carry hidden secrets deep inside.

Ever since he was young, Yaazer seemed larger than life. His walk was unique, distinguishing him from all others. He would gallop and jump in long strides, inspiring awe and amazement even before he was fully grown. He moved in a way that thrilled onlookers. From a distance, I would see his deportment and know it was him even before I could discern his features. His rich brown coat and proud stance gave him an aura of grandeur. We called him Yaazer when he was young and then changed his name to Dubai Millennium when he matured. He was a horse racing legend who captured my heart.

When he was two years old, I sent him to Newmarket in the United Kingdom to test him at the races on grass tracks. He spent the spring there and began to race at the beginning of October. He was amazing from the beginning. He participated in trial races in Doncaster and Goodwood, and won them all. These races prepare horses for the

Epsom Derby. Then he took part in the Queen Elizabeth II Stakes in Ascot and won that as well. He also won races in France, easily beating many well-known racehorses.

Dubai Millennium was a horse who liked to win, but he wanted to do so on his own terms. He would race as he deemed fit, without really heeding his jockey. He was different, and would run at top speed from the very beginning of every race. He liked to win, but with a slight twist; he loved to show off. He would break the resolve of his competitors from the very start. In fact, he would crush his opponents so badly they were unable to race in the same way again. He never raced as an equal; he always loved to stand out, as if he was asking all the other horses to follow him, and that broke their hearts!

Such a grand horse is suited for grand competitions. After having toured the racetracks of Europe, I decided to enter him in one of the world's biggest races, the 2000 Dubai World Cup, because he deserved to be the champion of all racetracks – both grass and dirt tracks. He was an exceptional horse who deserved to be the champion of the world.

The Dubai World Cup is an international event highly anticipated by horse lovers from all over the world. I relied completely on Dubai Millennium to win the race for me and personally supervised his transfer to Dubai, while also monitoring all the logistic preparations for the greatest event in horse racing. The pressure intensified as the race approached, until it was the eve of the long-awaited day.

> We called him Yaazer when he was young and then Dubai Millennium when he matured. He was a horse racing legend who captured my heart

I met with our jockey, Frankie Dettori, and gave him some important instructions on how to handle the horse. After Frankie left, I took a walk. Everyone had gone to sleep, which I greatly envied, for I was unable to find the peace and tranquillity to close my eyes. I went out to get a breath of fresh air, got into my car and headed to my favourite place – the stable in Al Qouz where Dubai Millennium was housed.

The other horses were getting ready to sleep or eating what was left of their food. As soon as I stopped my car in front of the stables, a head appeared above the door and I heard a soft neigh greeting me through Dubai's quiet, balmy night air.

I moved towards the door in the dark, without turning on the stable lights. Dubai Millennium was already calling me and guiding me in the right direction. It seems he was happy to see me that night. The night guards ran quickly towards the stable when they heard his hooves pawing, which stopped as soon as he saw my shadow moving slowly towards him. I was his usual visitor, especially at that time of night.

I slid the door open and entered the stall. He moved back slowly to allow me in. I gently touched his nose and then sat on the stack of hay that was beside him, my back to the wall. He let down his head gently and came closer, looking for his favourite food, which I always brought in my pocket.

I looked up at my huge horse who towered above me so proudly and asked, "How can you be so gentle Millennium?" He stopped and looked at me when he heard my voice, then went back to searching through my pockets. He knew, just as I did, that this was the eve of a

Dubai Millennium racing the wind

major race. He had been through this routine many times; the bandages that were wrapped around his legs, the number of times we had drawn his blood to make sure he was fit and how we watched over him when he left the stables in the afternoon. He noticed all this and knew what was going on. He was very intelligent and he knew that there was a big race awaiting him. Nevertheless, he did not really care: he was bigger than that.

I put my hand inside my pocket and gave him the carrot he was looking for. His ears moved back and forth as he listened to my voice. "My dear friend, I have been waiting for you all my life," I told him. I stopped talking for a while and remained still, then I went on, "Tomorrow is the day we've both been waiting for. This race means a lot to me, more than any other past race. Maybe you were more interested in other races, in Europe and other parts of the world, but this is my country. I want you to race here tomorrow, my friend – for me, for Dubai and for the Emirates."

He appeared to have understood what I was asking of him, because he took one step forward and put his nose close to my face. It was just for a few seconds but it seemed like an entire minute. Then he took a deep breath and whinnied. I put my hand on his snout to stand up; my visit with this regal creature had come to an end. I moved towards the door and opened it. Just before I went out, I turned around and smiled at him, and he turned to the window, relaxed.

Dawn broke on March 25th, 2000. It was the day of the Dubai World Cup; the event everyone had been eagerly awaiting. After a few quick morning meetings, I went on an inspection tour in the afternoon to

> His speed increased,
> like he was racing the wind.
> My heart pounded as I heard
> his hooves hit the ground
> like thunder

examine the security checkpoints for the race. I checked the helipads and the ambulances, and I went to the police office to review the emergency procedures with them. It was my duty to ensure the safety of Sheikh Maktoum, the Ruler of Dubai, as well as that of tens of thousands of people who would attend the race.

Time was moving slowly, and with each minute I grew more anxious. It was almost 5pm. Dubai Millennium was getting ready to leave the stables in Al Qouz to head for the racetrack in Nadd Al Shiba. I drove there and watched as he carefully entered the truck before the doors closed. He looked calm and confident. I followed the truck to make sure he arrived safely at his stable at the racetrack. Then I sighed deeply. Everything was up to him now.

The moment of truth had arrived. The track looked like a shining pearl set into Dubai, filled with thousands of spectators and fans. Many were looking forward to seeing Dubai Millennium race in the Dubai

World Cup for the first time. Frankie came to get his final instructions. I told him, "Do not fight the horse. If he wants to take off, don't hold him back; try and go along with his energy."

Everyone was tense, and from where I was sitting, I could see Dubai Millennium walking into the arena like a lion. His coat was shining, his eyes bright, and at that moment I felt that he was ready. He was like a warrior prepared and eagerly awaiting battle.

I held my breath as I saw the horses getting ready to take their places at the starting line. The commentator described the preparations of each of the racehorses, and the audience shouted as the gates opened. The horses were off!

Dubai Millennium got a good start out of the gate. The other horses obeyed their jockeys and slowed down after their initial burst of speed, which didn't bother Millennium. I saw Frankie try to reduce the horse's full-speed attack, but Millennium did not care. The jockey's attempts to slow him down were in vain. Frankie tried to sit as far back as possible on his back and put all his weight on his mouth to try and curb him. The horse just ignored him, speeding along like lightning until he was in the lead, totally ignoring any attempts to reduce the pace.

I heard the people around me commenting on the incredible speed at which Millennium took off; he ran as if his body was on fire. They began to curse Frankie and blame him for causing his horse to lose the race. Their voices grew louder, shouting, "What does he think he is doing?"

I saw Millennium was acting as if the track was a playground and began to wonder what such a take-off at top speed would mean for this race. As it continued, I asked myself, "What is he doing? Why is Frankie riding the horse at such a speed?"

Such an insane speed! Surely Millennium could not continue the race like that. The other horses were bound to catch up with him when he tired. My brother Sheikh Maktoum's consultants were screaming at the top of their voices, "This stupid jockey will make us lose the race. No horse, no matter how strong, can keep up this speed until the end of the race."

Sheikh Maktoum heard these comments, turned to glance at me, then went on watching the amazing show. Like me, he was a firm believer in my horse's abilities.

Although Millennium's performance defied all logic, I was sure he would win. He knew exactly what he was doing, because he was a horse unlike any other. He was very intelligent, so much so that when I sat with him the night before at the stable and told him how important this race was to me, he nodded his head in agreement. I could swear that this horse understood what I said. When he did not agree with me, he would raise his head and shake his mane in the air. He was my horse and my dear friend; I knew him well.

His speed increased, like he was racing the wind. My heart pounded as I heard his hooves hit the ground like thunder. When Millennium reached the straight part of the track, he covered it in very little time.

With Dubai Millennium after winning the Dubai World Cup in 2000

The audience was amazed, watching with bated breath to see what would happen next.

Millennium maintained his speed without tiring. Everyone thought it would be only a matter of minutes before he slowed down or even collapsed running to the finish line. Then the other horses would catch up with him. It would have been painful for me if Millennium tired and slowed, but instead he changed the way he was galloping and picked up even more speed. He ran on as if he was fleeing. The crowds were on their feet to witness this horse attack the finish line like a hurricane. Frankie stood in the stirrups and punched the air.

Millennium continued to run at full pace through to the line with the American thoroughbred Behrens only six lengths behind him, followed by the rest of the field the same distance back. Millennium had broken the track record. The audience went wild, overcome with excitement. Something rare, amazing and exceptional in the world of horse racing had taken place before their eyes.

I threw my race card up in the air and jumped for joy. I hugged my brother with an elation that cannot be put into words. We had the best horse and he had not let us down. The audience's chanting and enthusiasm were overwhelming. It was a win for Dubai, for the Emirates and for all Arabs. We owned the greatest horse in the world! It was like a dream coming true before my very eyes.

I patted my horse proudly, promising to reward him for his win later. I was still working at the time, and my priority was to make sure that Sheikh Maktoum was safe, as well as the audience that was so thrilled with Millennium's win. Despite my excitement, I could not stop scanning the area around me. In such situations, it would be easy for anyone to come close to my horse's hind legs and hurt him, or maybe, God forbid, hurt someone from the crowds that were flooding onto the racetrack. My mobile phone never stopped ringing that day; I couldn't answer all the incoming calls.

After celebrating with my family, my brothers, my daughters and my wife, I went back to my car and drove to a small villa where a group of my friends were gathered. I had barely stepped inside the villa when a man came and put his arms around my neck. It was my jockey, Frankie, who met me with an enthusiastic series of exclamations, "Sir, we won! Sir, we won! Where were you, sir? Where were you? We won, sir!"

Millennium refused to go
down like all the others. His
ending was a sad one, like
many champions in history.
The audience loves and adores
them, and they refuse to
depart in an ordinary way

That night, after everyone had calmed down, I went back to the stable in Al Qouz. "Thank you, my friend," I said to my horse. "You cannot imagine what this win means to me, dear Millennium." He nodded his head in agreement. He looked like he was turning his head, as if to welcome me. I put my hand inside my pocket and produced a carrot for him. After he ate it, he placed his nose on my arm like he would normally do to hear my voice while I spoke to him.

Dubai Millennium was different from any other horse. The jockey had to leave it up to him to act and not impede his style. He had to trust the horse to run the race as he saw fit. He was much faster than other horses, even without exerting any additional effort. Other horses simply could not keep up with such speed. Frankie always said that he was afraid to ride Millennium, not because he was a dangerous horse, but because he was such a strong one. Trying to control him was like trying to put reins on a rhinoceros. If he wished to run, nothing could stop him. Frankie always said he had never seen such a strong horse in his life, but this strength was not without control. Millennium knew exactly what he was doing; he knew he had to run from one point to another at top speed, and no one could stop him or curb his enthusiasm. His strength was exceptional and unlikely to ever be matched by another horse.

Millennium's reputation spread near and far in the world of horse racing. We filled his schedule with many events, and he won them all but one. He was the champion not only on grass tracks, but also dirt surfaces. He was the champion of every track upon which he set foot.

Fate dictates that a champion cannot remain a champion forever. The laws of nature say that what goes up must come down. Yet Millennium refused to go down like all the others. His ending was a sad one, like many champions in history. The audience loves champions and adores them. Champions refuse to depart in an ordinary way, but in a manner that immortalises them in the minds and hearts of those who love them.

On April 22nd, 2001, Millennium fell ill. On the following day, he had surgery for severe stomach pains, which led to complications. On April 24th, he was diagnosed with severe grass sickness. This is the last thing any owner wants to hear, for that disease is a death sentence. Grass sickness affects the nerves in a horse's digestive system and its body cannot fight it. Imagine! A handful of grass can topple a giant healthy horse.

On that awful Wednesday, I travelled from Dubai to Newmarket to find out if there was anything we could do. Unfortunately, his health deteriorated even further and he had a third surgery on Sunday, April 29th. Despite all the efforts we exerted with a team of the world's leading veterinarians, it was obvious that there was going to be no happy outcome.

I had to make the hardest decision that a horse owner ever faces, especially one who feels such deep affection for all horses as I do. Worse, this was the greatest horse in the world. It was such a painful decision but the most important thing was to end his suffering. Following the third surgery, I gave the order to let him die in peace. Dubai Millennium never woke up from that procedure.

I have still not woken up from the most beautiful dream I experienced with my friend, the greatest horse I have ever known.

48

The Prime Minister & Ruler of Dubai

I have been part of Dubai's government since 1968, and on December 2nd, 1971, I also became part of the federal government of the United Arab Emirates, when I assumed the role of Minister of Defence of the UAE. I accompanied Sheikh Zayed in the establishment of the Union, and Sheikh Rashid taught me a great deal about local governance. I have put everything I had into serving my country, my leaders and my nation throughout the years. I never competed for a role in government, nor did I ever aspire to be a ruler. In fact, I rejected the offered title of Crown Prince of Dubai four times. During my years of service, I was ambitious without being greedy, always striving to do something better for my country without usurping the rights of others. As I saw it, God had given me the responsibility of two families – my people and my actual family – and I worked my hardest to achieve their happiness.

January 4th, 2006, heralded shocking news. My brother, Sheikh Maktoum, God rest his soul, died suddenly from a heart attack. On that day, I became the Ruler of Dubai, and the rulers of the other emirates elected me Vice President and Prime Minister of the United Arab Emirates. The pain of losing Sheikh Maktoum was hard for me to bear. He died only 14 months after the passing of the father of our nation, Sheikh Zayed, may he rest in peace.

After their passing, I felt a greater responsibility before my God, country and history. I felt that the legacy they entrusted me with was too precious to neglect for even an instant. I started to think differently and my life began to change.

After I was elected, I retreated to be by myself. I prayed two 'rakats', or prayer cycles, to God, asking Him to inspire me and guide me towards the right path. I immediately began to organise my thoughts and priorities. I considered all the things that had been on my mind involving government reform. I made a list of candidates to form my new team and drafted a quick plan for my new work and way of life, trying to balance between my duties as Prime Minister and my role as the Ruler of Dubai and, with the grace of God, I embarked on this new life journey.

I formed a new Cabinet and wrapped up many of the committees in place at the time. I am not a strong believer in committees; I believe more in teams. I set up a new Prime Minister's Office and asked all the new ministers to draft clear working plans and strategies for the future. I set up a system to monitor the ministries' plans using 3,000 performance indicators. I paid off all the debts of the previous administrations. I felt that the work was being done systematically and that the wheels were beginning to turn. I asked all the ministers to accompany me on a retreat in the desert to discuss large-scale ideas. My aim was not just to get the wheels turning, but to propel our government to new heights.

We envisioned many great things for the future. A year after I became the Prime Minister, I convened a major event to which I invited the President of the United Arab Emirates, His Highness Sheikh Khalifa bin Zayed Al Nahyan and all the country's rulers, crown princes, ministers and officials, where I announced the strategy and vision of the Government of the United Arab Emirates. The President and the other rulers approved the new strategy, which aimed to make our government a best practice public sector by 2021, the year of the nation's golden jubilee.

Almost every month, I would announce a new system for government operations, with new indicators and goals. I followed up on their implementation, with a team assigned specifically for this purpose. Some of the ministers came to me and complained about the pressure, the increased workload, the numerous goals and the changes in the systems. I asked them to wait and bear with me. I then announced a Cabinet reshuffle, which introduced new blood with the energy necessary to continue the journey of meeting our ambitions and aspirations, and I thanked the former ministers for their service. I used to make changes to the Cabinet almost every two years to make sure that the team closest to me was always prepared and able to reach new heights. I also conducted a meeting for my ministers in which I asked each ministry to choose one or two indicators from international reports to which they would commit to ranking first in the world by 2021. They were surprised by this demand. Some of them asked me if they could be among the top ten rather than first, and many put together rationales for why this wasn't possible. I rejected all their excuses because I wanted to break the glass ceiling they had built for themselves. We are not less than others. Those who are in first place are not more efficient, intelligent or capable than we are. The ministers finally agreed to take on the challenge.

Today, before the deadline we set for ourselves, the UAE Government already ranks first globally in more than 50 international indicators, first regionally in more than 100 developmental indicators and is the most efficient in the world according to international reports. It ranks first in the world in enjoying the trust of its people. Sheikh Zayed, God bless his soul, always used to say something that I loved. He would say, "People pass and money passes. Only the homeland remains; only the things that we have done for our people will endure."

I wish Sheikh Zayed was still among us today to see what we have achieved in the UAE, which he built from nothing. I hope he knows that we are still keeping the vow we made to him and still travelling on the journey he started, in the same manner and with the same ethics and principles he instilled in us. I hope he is happy with what we have done. By the grace of God, we have realised many achievements through the spirit of cooperation and the complete conviction that we are capable. I made sure that my work teams and everyone else working with me in the government understood that there is no such word as 'impossible' in the UAE's dictionary.

I am convinced that the biggest obstacle preventing people from challenging the impossible is the belief that impossible exists, and the greatest achievement in empowering a person is instilling in them the concept that nothing is impossible. The best gift we can leave behind for future generations is teaching them to have the courage to venture where no one has dared to go before; to reach new heights that no one has thought of before.

I am a firm believer in this. I have invested extraordinary efforts in a particular project in order to break the glass ceiling that some people had built over their heads. I wanted to raise that barrier, or maybe even eliminate it for generations to come. I announced that we, the people of the United Arab Emirates, would send the first space probe to Mars in 2021, which is our golden jubilee.

The Mars Hope probe will travel 225 million kilometres before it reaches the orbit of the Red Planet, but we will get it there. And we will be one of only nine countries in the world to have done so. These countries may have started their developmental journey before us, but we are determined to beat them with our courage, speed and determination. The project has garnered much enthusiasm, bringing new life and energy to our community. Our youth are now looking to the heavens and our people now dream of reaching the stars.

My attempt to change the culture of the impossible in our society was a success. After I announced this project, I was very touched when a friend of mine told me, "If Zayed was here with us, he would be truly proud of us and would share in our happiness."

A meeting of the UAE Cabinet at the Louvre Abu Dhabi in 2017

49

Hope in
Humanity

During the ceremony honouring the winners of the Hope Makers Initiative in 2018

I enjoy hunting trips as they allow me to get out of my office, break my routine, renew my thoughts and recharge my energy. On a trip to a country in Africa a few years ago, we came to a small city where I had built a school for the local people. I made a surprise visit and found only a few dozen students occupying the large building that could hold many hundreds. I asked why this was the case, and was told that the main reason the children did not come to school was that they were starving. I was shocked by this justification. It took me a few seconds to comprehend. We build schools in order to eliminate hunger. Education is our main weapon against poverty, yet basic deprivation renders it useless in our hands. The world can sometimes be very cruel, making the poorest people suffer the most. They told me that the students went to farms to look for food every day, or stayed home if they were extremely malnourished and almost too weak to move.

I ordered a huge kitchen and canteen be built in the school, providing them with the best equipment, provisions and a full team to serve them. A year later, I went back and was pleased to find that the school had thousands of students attending in two shifts, morning and evening. I felt so happy. Giving to others blesses us in return with happiness, peace of mind and tranquillity. We are often more in need of giving than the needy are of receiving our aid. When you give to others, God gives to you. When you humble yourself, God elevates you. When you show mercy and compassion, God embraces you. I do not rely on my personal efforts to carry out humanitarian work, but on focused and sustainable organisations that are able to exert a greater impact and I have set up many projects that are managed by a highly dedicated team.

A few years ago I established Dubai Cares, a philanthropic foundation focusing on education in poor countries. It has benefitted more than

18 million students to date. Our initiatives also include a charitable organisation that has served two million families and the International Humanitarian City, which organises and supports rescue operations during natural and human disasters to a quarter of the world's countries. We have an educational foundation and a technical one that teaches programming to thousands. We have an endowment worth AED 1 billion for medical projects and research; an organisation that specialises in treating the blind which has served millions; an International Institute for Tolerance; conferences on culture and media; awards for the arts and the Arabic language, and many others. All of these operate under the umbrella of the Mohammed bin Rashid Al Maktoum Global Initiatives, which is comprised of more than 30 organisations and initiatives serving more than 130 million people.

I do not like to boast nor do I say this to enhance my reputation – God alone knows my intentions. I say this to encourage others who have the means to help. I tell them that their success in life should not impede their ability to look for the humanity in each and every person in the world. I have never heard of anyone who has been impoverished because they gave, who has had to stop working in order to do good or whose achievements were diminished because they gave to others. Everyone is capable of giving something. There is goodness in every person, and there is a merciful and generous soul inside each of us. Whenever you relieve the pain of another human, it is like planting a flower in a garden, lighting a candle in the dark or saving a life that God Almighty treasures.

In 2016, I launched a competition to prove that anyone can be a benefactor, regardless of their position or wealth. The average person can serve humanity just as well, or better, than thousands of business people who earn millions, because goodness stems from the heart, and compassion is part of the soul. This has nothing to do with how much money you have. I named the competition 'Arab Hope Makers', and called on anyone involved in humanitarian work to report their activities or nominate someone they knew to shed light on their noble efforts and award these hope makers, who spread goodness and help make life better for others, in front of millions of people in the Arab world. We received thousands of nominees, thousands of candles of hope lighting our region, most of whom were previously unknown. We heard so many inspiring stories; of the young man building orphanages in war-ravaged countries; the young woman who left her comfortable home in the GCC to live in an impoverished country for many years to save thousands of lives; the physician who put together a team of 3,000 doctors through social media to perform heart surgeries for children in impoverished countries; the young man who took in elderly homeless people and provided them with shelter and medical care from his own humble means; the young woman who saved desperate refugees from drowning at sea and the 70 year old lady whose age had not stopped her from travelling to and working for the poor.

These are just some of the stories we heard. I particularly remember Faris from Sudan. He was surprised to find that in some of his country's villages, school enrolment rates were extremely low because of hunger. Faris did not blame anyone for this. He did not speak of injustice, shed a few tears and then go back to his normal life. He went back home, and with the help of his mother he prepared sandwiches for the schoolchildren. The next day, he did it again, and soon the women in his neighbourhood were doing the same. A group of volunteers heard his story and they too began to help him. Over the course of ten years, they distributed more than 40 million sandwiches. All of this was done through a personal initiative that Faris started with good intentions, a good heart and very simple resources. Inside each of us there is a Faris.

When asked why I launched Arab Hope Makers, I said, "We are searching for the human inside every one of us." These models motivate ordinary people to be exceptional, they motivate the wealthy to realise that they can do more to help alleviate suffering and impoverishment, and they motivate everyone to think positively about the challenges facing their communities, instead of blaming them on external factors and waiting for the government to solve their problems.

A few years ago, we announced the Year of Reading in the UAE to encourage our children to read because reading broadens their minds and horizons and builds civilised, culturally nurtured personalities. I read in the news how little people in the Arab world read. I asked for suggestions, and one idea was to launch a competition called the 'Arab Reading Challenge', whereby participating students would read at least 50 books every year, and those who excelled would be awarded. The team suggested that we target 100,000 students every year to enter the competition, but I set the goal for the first year at one million. The reading challenge was launched, and that first year 3.5 million students participated.

During the second year, this number doubled to seven million, and in the third it rose to 10.5 million students from 44 countries around the

During the ceremony honouring the winners of the Arab Reading Challenge in 2018

world, each of whom read at least 50 books. It was a major achievement, but not one to lay at my door. All of the education ministries in the participating Arab countries were enthusiastic backers of the project. They believed in it, volunteered for it and motivated the students to participate. More than ten million students were monitored by 87,000 supervisors, all of whom were volunteers who had faith in this idea. You do not need much money to make an impact. All you need is a heart that is alive and compassionate, a will to detect those things which are not functioning properly and the courage to stand up to challenges so that this region can regain its civilisation. If each one of us gave a tenth of what we received, there would be no more poor, sick or illiterate people. I always remind my team that God is the Most Merciful and the Most Compassionate; our souls are from God Almighty, and the more merciful we are towards other people, the closer we are to God.

50

Ten Rules
for Leadership

A few months ago, I tweeted about one aspect of the crisis facing the Arab world. I said that our problem was administrative, not political, and that we needed administrators who are capable of bridging the developmental gaps in our region more than we needed politicians. I received this message on Twitter: "Your Highness, if you were to write the ten commandments of government administration addressed to an official in the Arab world, what would they be?"

I thought this was an excellent question and one that set my mind in motion: what are the ten most important rules for governance in our modern Arab world?

First and foremost, I maintain that life is a never-ending journey of learning. The more we learn, the more we realise how little we actually know, which is usually less than we imagine. Therefore, if we stop learning, we stop progressing in life. I have summarised my ten rules here for anyone holding an official post in government or administration, based on my own humble experience.

Rule 1: Serve the people. The purpose of government is to serve the people, the aim of public administration is to serve society and the role of government procedures, systems and laws is to serve human beings. Do not forget that. Do not glorify process, sanctify laws or think that systems are more important than people. They are there to serve the people, make their lives easier and more comfortable, and they can be changed at any time. Many lose sight of this and think that their role is to protect the systems that are in place, apply the provisions of the law literally and implement established processes. But this belief is the root cause of many of our administrative problems. If lawmakers, legislators, ministers, administrators, those who design and provide public services, as well as those who draft budgets and carry out projects, maintained sight of this ultimate purpose and upheld the 'serve the people' principle, their priorities, plans and decisions would change. There would be an administrative revolution in our Arab world.

Rule 2: Do not worship the position. Jobs, positions and responsibilities are all temporary. Your real value lies in the work you have done and your achievements. The harder you work, the more you accomplish; the more you elevate your status and name. You will be rewarded here in this world and in the hereafter. If you fall in love with the position, you will never have the courage to make decisions that will raise you to meet your ambitions. If you fall in love with the position, you will put it before your values, principles and aims you wish to achieve in serving the people. Make the position itself the least of your worries and you will be invigorated and inspired to change the organisation you work for, your community and your country. Look out for the welfare of your nation in the long run, and not for the seat which you temporarily occupy.

Rule 3: Set your plan. When you do not have a plan, you are setting yourself up for failure. Many officials go about their work on a daily basis, failing to look forward to and plan for the week or month ahead. This is one of the major administrative challenges we face. The role of a real leader is to know in which direction to go and guide the team towards it, motivating them to persevere until they reach their goal. If you fail to set a plan, you end up wandering aimlessly. It does not really make a difference whether you arrive or not, since you are not going to arrive at anything of any value.

Rule 4: Monitor yourself. Monitor the performance of your organisation. Assign a person to supervise it from within, as well as a neutral third party to assess it from outside. There must be clear performance indicators to ensure you are moving in the right direction to achieve the plan. Do not cheat yourself and your country by setting weak benchmarks and ineffective monitoring systems. It is impossible to achieve any project without real and honest indicators to bind yourself and your team.

Rule 5: Build your team. You cannot soar alone. A single hand cannot clap. Build a team that will elevate your objectives to new horizons. Delegate authority to them, guide them, teach them and empower them. Help the genius and the creativity inside them emerge, reward them and shine the spotlight on their achievements. Relax and enjoy the outcome, because a great team will take you to great places, while you will have to carry a weak team on your back until it breaks.

Rule 6: Innovate or leave. Governments that do not innovate get old and tired very quickly, unable to be a contender in the race. New ideas are an inspiration for constant renewal, which allow you to beat competitors, reduce costs and reinvent yourself. The new economy is based on innovation and the new world is on the lookout for new talents with fresh perspectives. Do not stop looking for sparks of genius among your team, your customers and the general public. There is nothing stronger than a great idea.

Rule 7: Communicate and be optimistic. Always communicate with the public, the community and the media around you. Build your image and reputation and tell the world about your ambitions and skills. Some governments think that communicating with the media is a secondary issue, and even consider it a nuisance at times. I tell you, it is essential and necessary. You build your image through the media, you establish transparency in your government and people will know where your administration is heading. Through the media, you can obtain the support of the people because they will know where you intend to take them. They will excuse you if you make a mistake, because they are accustomed to seeing you in their service. Declare your aims through the media and they will love you, and that will also be to your advantage because you will spare no effort to achieve those things which you have publicly committed to deliver. Always communicate, never hide. Treat the media as your friends, not your foes – they are friends to the dynamic honest achiever and enemies of the corrupt, shifty and lazy.

Rule 8: Compete. Competition is an essential trait of human behaviour. Compete with yourself and others. Companies succeed when they compete in an open environment. Strive for first place locally and internationally. Make sure your work environment is competitive. Compete with your past to build a better future. Compete with your goals to achieve more ambitious ones. Competition is a way of life in government, without it motivation will subside, enthusiasm will diminish and the flames of determination will die out.

Rule 9: Create leaders. When you create leaders, you create a future. A real leader is one who builds up other leaders, and a real organisation is one that produces leaders. Maintaining excellence lies in an organisation's ability to create leaders who can broaden horizons, bring more energy and take the organisation to new heights. The making of leaders is a secret granted only to those who have overcome their own ego and who understand that their greatest achievement is to build people, not edifices.

Rule 10: Go forth and live a meaningful life. Those of us working in government are blessed. Our jobs are not ordinary ones; they are the most beautiful things in our lives. They are life. Our jobs are meaningful; they enable us to change the lives of millions of people for the better. Never underestimate your role, your work or your efforts, for you are in the business of shaping lives, planning futures and building nations.

May God grant me and you the ability to serve the nation and its people.

This is only the beginning.

Mohammed bin Rashid Al Maktoum